For Craig
A Soto Sis forever!
Patti

A Year in the Life
of a
RECOVERING
Spendaholic

NO SALE

Patti Fralix

Patti Fralix

Write Way Publishing Company LLC

A Year in the Life of a Recovering Spendaholic

Printed in the United States of America

ISBN 978-1-946425-01-0
Library of Congress Control Number 2017937444

Cover design by Klevur

Book design by CSinclaire Write-Design

Write Way Publishing
Company LLC

Dedication

It is with sincere gratitude that I dedicate this book to my dear husband and best friend, Mike Fralix. Mike has been my best example of so many positive and good things. We have been married for almost thirty-three years. In these years, Mike has shown me unconditional love, which is the best human gift I have ever received.

Acknowledgments

It takes a village to do anything worthwhile in this life, and I am so blessed to have a wonderful village.

First and foremost, to Mike and our children, Tara and Chatham, and their spouses Stephen and Johnathan. You all mean the world to me. It grieves me that neither Tara nor Chatham have much interest at all in my "stuff," either now or when I am gone! And of course, to our three precious granddaughters: Mary Grace, Elsie, and Virginia. You are such a blessing to me. I will be so grateful if I live to see the wonderful young women you will become.

Also in the family category are Paula and MoMo, who during some of the years did more to raise Tara and Chatham to be the wonderful women they have become than anything Mike and I did. Paula and MoMo are more like oldest daughters and/or younger sisters. Your families, including Bryan, Patrick, and Bridget (Paula) and Mum Bernadette (MoMo) are also our family. Not to be forgotten is Uncle Barry, who continues to bring light and laughter to our gatherings. What a wonderful learning laboratory our family has provided me!

I also acknowledge the major role in my life and our celebrations of Mike's entire family, beginning with Dad and Rosie, sister Dianne and three brothers, Joe, Steve, and Phil, and their families. Our traditions would not be the same without all of you.

Next, to my friends who are my family. Judy and Pam, you are sisters. I would never have weathered the storms of my complicated life had you and your families not been there for me during those years. Through births, deaths, and divorce, you have been steadfast. I could not love you more if we were blood sisters. Also to Kathleen Harwell, another wonderful friend, and the one who stimulated my journey of finding my purpose and connected me to my need for beauty.

To Leah Friedman, a professional organizer (Raleigh Green Gables) who is a recent friend and a Solo Sister (women without siblings). Your influence inspired me to complete this book and to begin to finally get in control of my "stuff." You are a living example of the type of spender I want to become.

And to Gina. You were with me through the living and writing of this book and for many years before. I miss having you with me daily, but I know that you leaving me and the business was to live out your purpose, and I am so proud of you. We will be connected forever.

Finally, to Lee Heinrich. Your skill in all aspects of producing this book have greatly improved it. Had we met earlier, I am sure that this book would have been published when I planned for it to be. Or maybe not. Most likely we met exactly when we were meant to. As Dr. Elisabeth Kubler-Ross taught, there are no accidents; everything happens for a reason and is a part of the tapestry of our lives. (Mary Catherine Bateson.)

A final few words. In striving for authenticity, I worry that some of my words and examples may be "too close" for some people involved in or affected by them. While I tried to word my feelings and thoughts in such a manner to avoid hurting or disparaging anyone else, I may not have been totally successful. For any harm to others, which would be unintentional, I sincerely apologize.

— Patti Fralix, 2017

A Year in the Life
of a
Recovering
Spendaholic

Introduction

It is striking to me that the tenth anniversary of Hurricane Katrina in New Orleans has passed, and I am just now finishing my book about my year of no spending, a journey which began in New Orleans soon after Katrina. I never planned for it to take me this long to complete and publish this book. I finished at least 90 percent of the book while I "journaled the journey" that year and planned to publish it that next year. That plan did not come to fruition, and I have no reason for that other than I did not get it done. As I reflect on this, I am aware that this is a pattern with me, especially related to writing books. My first book, *How to Thrive in Spite of Mess, Stress and Less!*, was written over a period of six years. As I have gotten older, I have become more accepting of myself and no longer obsess over the "woulda, coulda, shouldas." In fact, in the case of my first book, I think the timing of its release made the message much more powerful than it would have been had I written and published it sooner. I wonder if the same outcome could happen with this book.

There have been many changes in our world in the past ten years. One of the changes is that many people in the U.S. are spending less on discretionary purchases, likely the result of the economic crisis our country suffered beginning in late 2008. I see this in many places, one being in my very small antiques and gifts business. Additionally, many people are expecting rock bottom prices for what they do purchase, and they are bargaining for lower prices much more now than ever before. These changes continue in spite of the fact that the economy has rebounded for many people. I don't expect the American consumer's purchasing habits ever to return to what they were before our latest major economic crisis.

As a result of my year of no spending, I have changed. I can identify three significant changes I have made due to the commitment to make no purchases for myself for a year. (For simplicity's sake, I refer to this as "no spending," although as you read the book, you will see that I did spend on limited "disposable" things for myself that year.)

The first change was making a commitment, not just a plan or a goal. Making a year-long commitment meant a good time frame for the change to really cement in me—not thirty days or ninety days, but a full year. Ten years later I am even more convinced that this was a good decision. Lasting meaningful change requires a long-term commitment.

The second change is that I am no longer an impulsive buyer; usually, that is. I am not perfect; old patterns do die hard, even with a commitment. But more often than not, I am able to walk away from a purchase I did not plan to make, knowing that the item will usually be there later if I still want it, and if it isn't, I have learned to be ok with that. Due to my year of not spending and the years since, I am a much more mindful buyer, which was part of my long-term goal.

The third change is that I do not waste money. At least I do not waste money on purchases. For example, one small practical change is the practice of taking my own homemade iced tea with me when I am driving instead of stopping and purchasing a beverage that will not be as good as what I can prepare myself. I realize this change is not major, but it is a positive change in attitude and practice and one I am proud to have made. Because it is both an attitude and a practice change, it does not just relate to a beverage decision but also touches other decisions as well.

Changes I have **not** made need to be mentioned as well as I want to be totally transparent with myself and my readers. I still purchase too many things, and some of them are things that I do not need. Avoiding this behavior was better the first and even the second year after my year of no spending. After that my spending gradually increased, although not to previous levels. I am still a spendaholic, and since this is an addiction, I probably always will be. I am, however, no longer a shopaholic. I do not shop for diversion, out of boredom, or to satisfy other needs. This fact alone—that I am not shopping as often—means I do not spend as much as I once did. I have not replaced shopping in a physical store or mall with shopping online, replacing one shopping *medium* with another.

But I do buy too much on credit and have not been concerned with the increasing amount of credit card debt until recently. I know credit card debt results in me wasting money, perhaps as much or even more than if I still purchased at previous levels. Lately, I have changed this. I have stopped adding to my credit card debt. My commitment now is not to buy anything on credit that I do not have the money to pay for when the credit card bill is due. This will probably be an even tougher challenge than the year of not spending. It may, in fact, be another year of not spending!

As I am reflecting on my changes, I can think of one more change I made from my year of not spending. I am making a slow move to what is usually referred to as minimalism. The focus of minimalism that I ascribe to is the one promoted by Joshua Becker. This minimalism is not about deprivation but is about living with less. Leah Friedman, who owns an organizing business and whom I am proud to call friend, has been a major influence in this journey of mine. Leah's philosophy is that organizing does not include buying more containers to put more stuff in, but getting rid of stuff we don't need and then making sure we bring less stuff in. I have begun this journey and am making slow progress. I plan to make this a commitment in 2017.

Change is difficult, especially when it requires we change ourselves in fundamental ways. Making a true *commitment* to the change is an important first step, but this time I want to go a step further, so I am taking a somewhat different approach to my 2017 commitment than I did to my 2006 commitment. I recently have learned about personal, social, and structural changes that can be made to make it easier to maintain the change commitment. I discovered this approach from a book published in 2011 titled *Change Anything*, by authors Patterson, Grenny, Maxfield, McMillan, and Switzler. I highly recommend this book to anyone wanting to change anything. It debunks the importance of willpower in changing behaviors and puts the attention on six sources of influence working with us or against us to make a change. This is a powerful book, and I recommend it highly to those wanting to change.

My hope for my readers is that my book, *A Year in the Life of a Recovering Spendaholic,* will provide some useful insights with the small steps and incremental attitude adjustments that happened along the way on my personal journey. This is by no means a "how to change" book or even "how to spend less money" but rather is more of a "walk with me" as I endeavor to make a significant attitude and practice change in my own (admittedly comfortable) life, especially in my spending habits, small and large. I am aware that this book does not deal at all with issues that many in our society struggle with, such as not having sufficient food, clothes, or shelter. That is not my level of financial focus. I have been truly blessed with good jobs all of my adult life that have been financially lucrative and a wonderful husband who also has had good jobs that have provided a better than average income. We have not known the financial struggle that many in our society deal with daily. We have been truly blessed. Regardless, I have not managed my money well. I have usually spent more than I have made, or better said, I have not managed my money sufficiently to know what I have or don't have.

When I made this commitment in late 2005, I decided to change my spending habits. I knew that I needed to do so, and for the first time in my life, I was ready to do so. I faced that fact that I am a spendaholic and wanted to change that.

Regardless of our spending level or ability, if we spend without attention to the amount of money we have, we have a spending problem. If this is an issue with you, and you want to improve, this book can inspire and perhaps help you.

I welcome your feedback, ideas, and suggestions as I continue this lifelong journey to be a responsible spender.

My journey began ten years ago. I expect that it will continue for many years to come and will evolve as I do.

December 2005

December 29

It really started months ago as an isolated thought that I should stop spending. My thoughts were to stop spending for a week, or a month, maybe even three months. But today on December 29th, the thoughts changed. Today, I am making the decision to stop spending for one year. Where I am as I make the commitment to carry out this change is important.

My husband and I were in New Orleans with friends, walking in the French Quarter, venturing into different shops. It was just a few months after Hurricane Katrina, the largest natural disaster in U.S. history. We have always loved New Orleans and decided to spend a week in the Big Easy between the Christmas and New Year's holidays. We weren't sure what we would find when we arrived, but we just wanted to go there. I certainly had no thoughts to change my life on that trip, but that is exactly what happened.

We were walking along Royal Street, the posh shopping area in the city. As a result of Hurricane Katrina and its effects, many stores and businesses had closed, some likely never to reopen, but many others displayed hopeful "opening soon" signs. There were still others that were not only open but seemed to have lots of "stuff," much of it very expensive. The window in one shop, the one where a guard greets you at the door, had a set of silver flatware in a massive wooden box priced at $98,500. There were also t-shirt shops, praline shops, and many art galleries. Even with many shops closed, the choices of things one does not need and may in fact already have, (and yet like me, probably can't find!) to spend on seemed overwhelming.

The dichotomy of the scene and circumstances, devastation and opulence, destroyed businesses and thriving operations, started me thinking about my spending. Thoughts of the Christmas that had just passed went through my mind, and I remembered that I had presents that I never got around to wrapping. It seemed that the season was like the year, gone oh so quickly. I began to think of my life and had the desire that it not go by so fast. I realized that I had little to no control over the length of my life, but I could take better control over how I would live it. And as for "spending," for too many years my spending habits have been out of control. Although what I spend money on (actually, too often, what I buy with plastic) varies, the fact is that I spend too much. I had no real plans to change that when we arrived in New Orleans. But I did.

At that moment, December 29th, on Royal Street in New Orleans, I faced the fact that I have a spending addiction, that I am a spendaholic. I also, for the first time, wanted to do something about it, something drastic. I wanted to stop spending for the entire next year. I verbalized my thinking to my husband Mike and friends, and Mike latched onto the idea with an excitement that surprised me.

One of the most interesting aspects of his response was that he thought I could do it. He started talking about how this could be the idea to propel me to greatness, one that could even land me on Oprah! We started talking about different aspects of "no spending" and what it would look like. The more we talked, the stronger my commitment became. I began to get excited about the plan, and ideas began to gel. I realized that this decision could very well be the most important tangible way that I could "walk my talk." This could be a way that I could live my business tagline "Inspiring Positive Change." Perhaps my change could inspire positive change in others and help them to be their best, whatever that is for them. Helping others to be their best is my passion and is the core basis for my speaking and consulting business. It also could be an example of Gandhi's wise saying, "You must be the change you wish to see in the world."

Although those thoughts are going through my mind, I am very clear that while this change could create congruence for me and those I serve, this change first and foremost is for me and no one else. If others get inspired, that is great, but that isn't the reason for the decision. I am taking responsibility to change what *I* need to change.

So here I am, making my decision here and now and putting it in writing to stop buying "stuff" for an entire year. This will be my definition of "stuff": clothes, furniture, all personal items, and even books. "Stuff" also includes things for our home, one of my main spending categories. I know this will not be easy, that, in fact, it will often be painful for me. But for some reason, it is something that I now desperately want to do. For all of 2006, I will not buy any personal "stuff," regardless of the reason.

As I am thinking this through, I decide my plan will include purchasing appropriate items for other people. For occasions such as birthdays, I will search my well-stocked gift closet before purchasing additional gift items. (The gifts in my gift closet were purchased at different times, usually when they were on sale or when I found the "perfect" gift for someone. They are *not* "re-gift" items.)

While I have not yet formulated all aspects of this plan, there are other "givens." I will spend on services, such as hair care, but I will spend more wisely and be more respectful of not being wasteful. I will not add any new purchases, such as hair care products I am not currently using. I will replace only currently used general health and beauty products.

I will spend for things for my core business, speaking and consulting, but much more deliberately as I continue to grow the business. I will also buy things for resale for Traditions, my small antiques and gifts business, but again, much more deliberately.

While these thoughts and decisions are whirling through my head, I am going to allow myself to buy whatever I want the last two days of this year. I don't have anything particular in mind to purchase, other than replacing a pair of shoes. I am mentally adding that once January comes, whatever shoes I have in my closet will have to suffice, for part of this plan is to make use of what I already have. Before this year of no-spending pain begins, I want to enjoy a last bit of spending freedom. I am thinking of other things that I might want to buy these last two days of spending.

December 30

I surprised myself by making only two small purchases today. I bought a book (*Being Dead Is No Excuse* by Gayden Metcalfe). Giving up purchasing books for a year will be one of the hardest things as books are one of my most frequent purchases. When I mentioned to Mike that not buying books for a year will be hard for me, he asked if I have books that I haven't read. I replied, "of course." Mike said, "Can you read those?" Of course, I can. I have often found books at home that I have bought and not read and wondered when I would get around to reading them. They will be on my 2006 reading list. He also mentioned the library. I don't think that I have been to a library in twenty years, but the prospect of reconnecting with libraries is a pleasant thought. Also, some of the time that I would spend reading, I can spend doing other things, such as writing. Hmmm.

The only other purchase that I made today was a $3.00 pair of earrings that were on sale from $15.00. I also tried on a pair of diamond earrings that were priced at $25,000. The salesperson said that I could have them for $19,500 and save $2,000 in sales tax if I had them shipped home! They were lovely, and I would love to have them, but they are not in the spending plan for '05, '06, or any year that I can foresee. But then, maybe if I spend more wisely, someday I may be able to buy things of that value. Now, wouldn't that be great?!

December 31

I tried to find something that I really wanted and that wasn't frivolous to buy today, but I couldn't. Perhaps this new commitment has already affected my spending thoughts. Although I saw many things to purchase, the desire to buy on this last day of a spending year was subjugated to being mindful of my spending. I bought two items, a t-shirt for granddaughter Mary Grace and a New Orleans 2006 Datebook. It seemed a fitting purchase to chronicle this coming year in a New Orleans date book since this is where my commitment to changing my spending habits and my new life will begin.

First Quarter 2006

January 1

Today is the first day of my year of no spending. I plan to use this book to chronicle the successes and struggles I likely will have, including the thoughts and feelings that accompany the decisions I make. I will journal my thoughts and feelings at least weekly.

January 2

Our friends left New Orleans this morning. We said goodbye to them, then went to breakfast, and are now back in the hotel. Mike and I have no plans but to relax. My head is full of ideas about more of the specifics for my no-spending plan.

I will live on a budget, spending mainly cash other than for necessary business expenses. Since I will not be spending on "stuff," I will have some money left over at the end of each month. That money will be equally divided between debt repayment and savings. I am designating the savings for me to spend in the following year.

This latter is my incentive to remain committed. I do believe in incentives. I know that there are going to be times that this plan will feel like an albatross around my neck. I hope the thoughts of delayed gratification will help me get through those times. I confess I am not usually very good at delayed gratification, but if I can curtail frivolous spending for this year, I believe that I will create more mindful spending habits for my future.

If I thought this new decision would put a permanent moratorium on my spending, I doubt that I would be able to keep the commitment past today. On the other hand, if I merely consider this just a year of no spending without creating any real change likely for subsequent years, why go to this effort for the year? Surely not just to prove that I can do it. If I am going to go through a year of no spending, I do need to anchor the plan to a spending attitude (and life) change.

While it was momentarily hard to walk by the storefronts in New Orleans this morning and know that I was not going to buy anything, the no-buying decision was easier when I remembered the visit to St. Bernard's Parish yesterday.

St. Bernard's Parish is one of the areas hardest hit by Hurricane Katrina and the subsequent break of the levees. The area is like a third world country or a ghost town. Four months later, there are still no services, not even electricity and water, in this area. Miles upon miles of devastation were evidence of nature's wrath and the impermanence of "stuff." Any of the "stuff" that remains after the devastation is unusable. A strong realization swept over me that "stuff" is far less important than *homes*, which are different than *houses*, most of which were destroyed, and family, all of whom are displaced, separated, or worse, their lives were lost in the storm and aftermath. If there is anything in those devastated areas worth rescuing other than people, it would be any photographs or memorabilia that somehow managed to survive. Perhaps from those small pieces of "before the storm," the displaced can create a semblance of home with or without houses. Now *that* is suffering. Going a year without buying "stuff" is merely a minor inconvenience in comparison.

January 3

Working on taxes all day today reinforced the decision to quit spending. It is amazing how much money went out in comparison with how much came in. This year will definitely be a year of financial recovery.

January 5-6

Mike and I flew from New Orleans to Atlanta to spend a couple of days with granddaughter Mary Grace and then went on to visit family and friends in Alabama. Shopping wasn't even missed!

January 7

We are back home in Raleigh and traveled to Southern Pines to celebrate the 75th birthday of a friend. We met many wonderful friends and family members of the birthday honoree. "It's a small world" and "six degrees of separation" were the words of the day as connections were made with people we had never met before, but who are connected to others in our lives, past and present. Again, I did not miss shopping, and the paramount importance of relationships was reinforced as we experienced this celebration. I feel a pattern developing. Relationships can be more satisfying than the temporary thrill of shopping.

Mike and I and a family friend took our youngest daughter Chatham out to dinner to celebrate her return to graduate school. I spent my first money of the New Year on dinner. That money comes out of my monthly allowance. Since I did not have cash, I charged it, but I will put the money in an envelope so that when the bill comes in, the money is there to pay for it. No more surprises on the credit card!

January 8

Mike and I traveled to Tampa, Florida, for a business meeting. As long as I stay in the air, this year of no spending is easy!

January 9

Mike and I drove to Ocala, Florida, to have breakfast with his Dad and Rosie. Rosie is Dad's second wife. Mike's mom died in 2000, and Dad was grief stricken and so lonely. We were glad when he and Rosie found happiness together and married soon thereafter.

We drove a total of four hours to meet with Dad and Rosie in Ocala, and it was well worth it. The breakfast was good, but the nourishment of being with family for even a little while was the wonderful part. We are not unaware that with Dad being 82, opportunities to be with him should never be taken for granted. A family friend joined us, traveling up from Orlando. Mike shared my no-spending plan with them. The more people who know, the more the commitment is cemented!

I was out of town last week when I realized that I had not purchased the book for this month's book club. Given my decision not to buy any books this year, it was necessary to find another way to acquire it or skip book club. Since I was out of town, the library wasn't an option. Or was it? Time to problem solve. I asked my assistant, Gina, if she had a library card, to which she replied, "I haven't been to a library in years; I don't even know where a library is in Raleigh!" It was then that I discussed my plan with her, and asked if she would see if the library had the book I needed, get a library card, and pick it up for me if they did. They did, she did, and now Gina is a card-carrying patron of our local library, and I saved thirteen dollars and eighty-six cents! First test passed, thank goodness! (And I know they won't all be this easy.) While Mike drove us to and from Ocala, I was able to finish the book in time for book club.

January 10

I wasn't the only one at book club tonight who had a library book. In fact, someone noticed my library book and that generated discussion about different libraries. Instead of feeling book-deprived, I felt quite mainstream!

January 11

I made my first trip to the mall today. I needed face powder and had several coupons to "cash in" for the purchase. My out of pocket expense for the powder was less than fourteen dollars. My only other purchase was for a planner refill, a business purchase, which cost nineteen dollars.

I felt quite in control of my spending and did not really "want" for anything. What a different feeling from overspending, regret, guilt, shopping to ease the pain of the guilt, and the cycle starting all over again.

January 12–13

Today, I did a massive cleaning out of "stuff" and marveled at how much I have. Most of this stuff I have had for quite a long time, much of it I have not used in many years, and some of it I probably will never use. I packed up some things for Goodwill, some for the antique shops, and threw away some of the stuff that I determined no one would want. I am committing to myself that by the end of 2006 if I have not worn or used what remains, I will get rid of it. The challenge is on to make good use of the things that I have been holding on to so dearly, or they will be gone forever!

In the category of spending, I went out to a nice dinner with a friend and spent $47.32, which I put on a debit card and which will come out of my allowance.

January 14–15

Mike and I went to the beach and had a very peaceful weekend. We detoured through Sanford, NC, on the way back to Raleigh to show our respect at a good friend's daughter's visitation. Our friend's daughter was 43 years old when she lost her one-year battle with cancer. Being there for a friend—*that* is important.

We came back to Raleigh and went to dinner at our local "Cheers," Sawmill Tap Room. I treated at dinner; the tab was $34.74; again, out of my allowance.

It occurs to me that I am spending most of my allowance on eating out. I guess that is to be expected, since I can't spend on much else! Now, let me re-frame that. It isn't that I "can't" spend (and I know I am fortunate in that), but instead, I am choosing to spend much more deliberately and wisely. And yes, also, to spend much less!

January 16

I went to Belk's for the big President's Day sale. I needed hose for business attire, and they were 20% off. I really did *need* them. I had searched my dresser drawers and found no suitable hosiery. I bought enough to last me all year and used the coupons. I saved more than I spent! Now, I know that you have heard that "saved more than I spent" before, but this time it is true. Again, what I spent (approximately twenty dollars) came out of my allowance.

I met Mike and business colleagues for a business dinner this evening. Thank goodness for a business dinner; I did not have to spend any of my allowance for this meal!

January 17

Another meal! A friend and I went out to dinner. My tab was $18.69, which I put on my debit card, and you guessed it—it came out of my allowance!

As I think about all the meals out I have been enjoying, it is no wonder that my Weight Watchers weigh-ins aren't going very well.

I am realizing that eating out is more about the social aspect than the food. I believe some of that comes from my childhood. There are many memories from my childhood about food. I do not remember ever having a meal sitting down together at a table at home with my mother. I had many meals by myself at home, but none with her, at least none that I remember. Too often she drank her meal. And there was no father in the picture.

The meals that I did have at home were usually frozen TV dinners. Fresh, home cooked food was not my mother's specialty. I did have a fair share of home cooked food, however, since I had two southern grandmothers. That food was no healthier than the frozen TV dinners though given it was mostly the unhealthy Southern cooking favorites!

It is no wonder that food, and meals out, have a very special significance for me, and it isn't just about the food. Food apparently had/has a special significance for me. Food is nurturing, and I certainly lacked nurturing as a child. There were two times in my life that I remember family that felt nurturing. First there were the years that I lived with my Aunt Bebo and Uncle Barry. We had good meals and family time, although much of it was chaotic. I felt loved during those years and was grateful for the haven they provided me from my mother's troubled life.

The other time in my childhood that I felt nurtured by family and food (not biological family, but chosen family this time) was when I was at home with Jean and Marshal Jackson, who were my church youth leaders and who cared for me as their own during my preteen and teenage years. They were my stability during those years. I learned about the combination of love and food and sharing them with others from Jean and Marshall, lessons that I try to live in my adult life.

With food such an issue for me, it is no wonder that I was overweight for many of my teenage years. Judging from pictures, I was also very sad for some of those years. All of this probably had something to do with the poor choices I made as a young adult. Thank goodness those poor choices were ones that did not include drugs (legal or otherwise) or alcohol.

Looking back, it is amazing that I did not start drinking at a young age. My maternal grandfather, who died when I was young, was an alcoholic. My mother and legal father were both alcoholics, although to my knowledge neither admitted it, and both were "functioning" alcoholics. Had I engaged in teenage drinking like many other young people, I might have wasted my teenage years, and my life could have involved the choices (or circumstances, some of both, really) my mother made. And the problem for me could have been, if I had indulged in those behaviors, that I might not have been able to go to college. I knew education, especially college, was my ticket out of the unhealthy social environment in which I lived for many of my childhood years. Seeing the negative effects of drinking, I just had no interest in alcohol.

Illegal drugs were not common in my social circle in high school and college. I had no interest in drugs either (illegal drugs or drugs of any kind for that matter). I think the influence of my fundamentalist religious paternal grandparents and maternal grandmother was the deciding factor in my direction rather any influence of my peers. My grandparents were my only stability, and I never wanted to disappoint them.

The trend today seems to be to medicate all conditions, including apparently equating temporary sadness and common coping problems of adolescence as clinical depression needing chemical treatment. Fortunately, this was not the case during my younger years, or I might have found myself "zoned out" on legal drugs. I really worry about young people today. Too often at the first sign of problems, they are rushed off to counselors who are too quick to prescribe medication. Or at whatever age, people decide to self-medicate with either alcohol or drugs. (Well, apparently, my brain transitioned into my "professional" thinking mode as I am writing this, and I think I am looking down from my high horse! I still want to add one more thought on this subject then I'll move on.)

Thinking back to my youth, considering both every day growing up and the effects of alcoholism in my family, I am compelled to encourage parents to spend more time with their children. Get them away from TV, computer, and all technology. Have quality family time. If children or adults truly are depressed, then medication may be an appropriate part of the solution. I would never discourage the use of counseling and appropriate treatment, but I do believe that the medication part of the solution is sometimes selected too quickly today. I think sometimes medication is used as a substitute for the love, time, and attention that children and young people need, which they can get, hopefully, from their parents, but if not, then from other loving family members. In many cases today, as in my past, it does take a village!

January 18

Mike is out of town, and I am eating at home tonight, cooking my dinner from a recipe that I received at Weight Watchers last week. This is much less expensive than eating out. In fact, this meal costs me nothing since groceries are a line item in Mike's budget!

January 20–22

Mike and I were at Oak Island, NC, for the weekend, which is where we spend most weekends when we are not traveling for other reasons. We have a condo there and an investment that consumes much of Mike's time. We, along with some others, bought the Oak Island Golf Course about eighteen years ago, purely as an investment. For all years but the very first year, Mike has been Chairman of the Board, which requires that he/ we spend a lot of time there taking care of the business.

A few years ago, I rented space in an antique shop in Southport, the adjacent town, to give me something to occupy my time while Mike spent so much time on golf course business. It has worked. I love being at Oak Island; it has become our second home. We usually eat at our restaurant at the club, and this weekend was no exception. The only difference this time is that I am on a different spending plan. The meals that I eat out are now my responsibility, not Mike's. This weekend was expensive! My food costs for the weekend totaled almost $100.00. Wow! That is a hefty portion of my $775.00 monthly allowance. I am not so sure that the food was worth it.

My plan for January has been to stay on my budget while not creating too much change in my regular activities. Primarily, I want to see where my money goes. Much of my money is obviously going to eating out. I may want to change some of that in February.

This weekend a good friend's father died. "Father Fred" lived a good 82 years. My friend Maureen is really more like a family member than a friend since she has been so close to our family for almost twenty years. She is very fortunate to have had such a wonderful father. Father Fred will be sorely missed.

I wonder what my life would have been had I had a "Father Fred." I don't even know my biological father. I found out after my mother's death in 1998 that my legal father is not my biological father, something that I had suspected for years. I was also told who my biological father is, at least supposedly. I made contact with him, and he denied it.

Perhaps there is a relationship to money and food to be found somewhere in my family issues. Even so, let me now and forever get over them. At 54 years of age, it is not necessary to use childhood issues as excuses for current problems.

Easier said than done.

January 23

I spoke in Greensboro, NC, this morning. Greensboro is approximately an hour and a half from my home and office in Raleigh. Driving back, I stopped for gas before I needed to when I saw gas for almost ten cents a gallon less than it is in Raleigh. Previous to this life change, I would have waited until I was past empty since I hate to stop for gas. By stopping when my tank was three-fourths empty, I saved two or three dollars. Since my driving pattern requires at least one tank of gas a week, my decision to now fill my gas tank when I find lower priced gas will save me (conservatively) $120 a year. And for no real effort. You may be thinking, "big deal." Well, it *is* a big deal. It is a decision that if made in a variety of other ways will add serious money to my balance.

I had an additional (minor) moment of victory. Although I was thirsty, I decided to wait until I got home to have a soda, saving more than a dollar. I am learning to respect delayed gratification, something that has always been a problem for me and something that surely has had a direct impact on my excessive spending. Although this is true, I am struck by the dichotomy of this compared to what I spent on food this past weekend.

I spent almost $100 on two meals yesterday, and would not spend a dollar on a soda today!

I am noticing that I do this fairly frequently. I spend too much on some things, then scrimp small change and think that I am being frugal. Am I being frugal, or am I kidding myself? Both, I think. While I do need to spend less on food overall, I am willing to spend on quality food that I enjoy. And, yes, I am proud of the fact that I could control my desire for a soda and wait until I returned home and had lunch, even if all that decision saved was a dollar. Dollars do add up but the big gain is practicing the delayed gratification and exercising control over a spending decision.

My take away from this thought process is that as long as I stay within my budget, I can spend exactly the way I am spending. I just may have to spend less often. That means over time I will be spending less and making wiser decisions on what I buy.

Hopefully, that is. The end of the month is only a week away, and I can see already that I will not have any money left over and will even have to spend less than I have been spending these other three weeks. There are also some unanticipated expenses, so I might even run out of money! I am going to Canada for the services for my friend's father. While lodging and food will not cost me any money there since I am staying with friends, there are charges and taxes on the "free" award airline ticket. And I will want to show my appreciation for the family's hospitality in some way, either while I am there or soon after I return home. Then there is the funeral acknowledgment, flowers or a contribution to a charity in memory of the deceased. These are important since Mike and I believe strongly in showing our respect in situations such as this. Mike would say that unanticipated things always come up and that I need to prepare for them by saving. I believe this as well; I just have not done it. So, here is the first month of my new plan, and I haven't been able to save yet, so what shall I do? The obvious thing is that if I go over my budget this month, I must make that up in subsequent months. Given this, perhaps it is best to budget monthly and quarterly, spending less in some months in the quarter when I have spent more in others. I will ask Mike what he thinks since he is clearly better at this than I am.

January 26

I am on the plane returning from Canada back to Raleigh. The services for Father Fred were well attended, which is evidence of a life well lived and a person loved and respected. It was nice to meet some of the family I had not met.

My spending was as I expected. The only money that I spent was for dinner. I picked up the check for five of us as a token of my appreciation for the hospitality of my host. The "five" included my friend and her mother. This was the right thing to do so I view it as a good spending decision. The bill was $169. That, along with the $100 memorial contribution, and the $86 taxes for my plane ticket, puts a sizeable hole in my monthly budget. It will be necessary to make this up in this first quarter, regardless of Mike's opinion. Mike will want to share these expenses with me, but I do not know to what degree. Since I made most of these decisions without discussing the details with him, I will be prepared to accept what he chooses to contribute, down to and including nothing. I know that he will be supportive, including financially, but I may have spent more on some of the particulars than he would have.

I feel somewhat "crass" adding up the amount of money spent

on funeral acknowledgments. But Mike has always said that there is only so much money to go around, regardless of how important or worthy the cause for which it is spent. Maybe I am finally accepting the validity of this. Why did I not learn these lessons at 24 instead of 54?

The answer to that question is most likely found in this book.

I resisted purchasing anything in the Toronto airport, deciding that I could wait. Why spend two to three dollars for a soda at the airport just because I have an hour wait before the plane departs? Too often I have eaten or had something to drink just to fill the time. That is eating or drinking out of boredom more than hunger or thirst. Plus, there will be complimentary beverages and snacks on the airplane and in the Delta Crown Room when I get to New York. I decided to wait.

These may be small changes, but I am proud of my progress! I would never have thought of these things before. Interestingly enough, I have $200 cash in my purse, so it isn't that I don't have the money. In fact, I have more money in my wallet and am spending less than when I had no cash and spent anyway. Is there a message here? Yes, I think so!

And only five more days to go in this first month of my new life. I am looking forward to tallying up at the end of the month although I do not anticipate any surprises. You don't really have surprises when you stay on top of your finances regularly.

January 30–February 1

I made a quick road trip to Georgia to see granddaughter Mary Grace, and of course, her parents, daughter Tara and son-in-law

Stephen! I have pledged to myself to see her at least once a month, and twice a month when possible. She is almost a year old and changing so fast. Watching her grow is the best example of how quickly time flies and that lost time can never be regained or re-lived.

And I am 1/12 of the way through my year of financial recovery!

The only money that I spent was for gas and less than $3.00 for food. On many other visits I have taken us all out to dinner and had budgeted to do so this trip, but Tara cooked dinner both nights. We enjoyed family dinner in the dining room, which made me so proud of Tara and Stephen. So many families rarely sit down to a meal together, much less a home cooked meal served in the dining room on a weeknight. If you have read this far, you know how important family meals are to me. And it really is about more than the food.

February 2

A challenge presents itself. Mike is having his management retreat at our house next week. Eleven people will be spending two days at our dining room table. The table is wood and needs to be covered to function as a "work" table. The only tablecloth that we have for the table when it is fully extended is a double damask from Ireland, which I (and Mike, for that matter) would not want to be a base for his group's work. The table will need to be fully extended for 11 people. What am I, or we, to do about this challenge?

I asked Gina to call around and get prices on a durable table-cloth that is large enough for the extended table. She found one at Williams Sonoma. Now, what to do? Remember that I can't buy anything for myself or the house for this entire year! Well, this tablecloth isn't for me or the house; it's for Mike's work group. Mike was out of town when I realized that we have this dilemma, and I decide that I should be able to solve this problem. I recognize that although too often I make decisions that obligate Mike and me financially, I see only two practical ways to solve this particular problem. (What is *not* an option is to have the 11 people working on our dining room table for two days without the table being protected.)

One option is that the cost of the tablecloth is a part of the cost of the meeting and that this is legitimate and reasonable since the company is not paying any facility cost to host their meeting at our house. Mike can choose to expense the cost of the tablecloth if he is comfortable with that, including that the company can own the tablecloth. Another option is that Mike's Valentine's present to me is a tablecloth! His choice! I know of no other option that would allow me to maintain my resolve not to buy anything for me or our house.

Mike agreed. He decided that giving me the tablecloth for Valentine's Day was the best of the two options regarding the uncovered table dilemma.

This situation is probably like many others that I encounter in a year. What is different is that I came up with solutions that didn't cost me any unbudgeted money and yet met the needs at the time.

There are often solutions to our challenges, especially when we think creatively.

February 3

I made myself weigh in at Weight Watchers today and had lost .8 of a pound. I am going up and down one to two pounds most weeks. At this pace, the last eight pounds are coming off very slowly. I need to write down what I am eating. I know that keeping the facts in front of me helps me to stay on track with my eating. The same is true of managing my money.

Today, I resisted buying a box of WW snacks. I decided that $7.50 for them was not good value. They are good, but not that good. Just because they were lining the shelves as I weighed in, and even though I was hungry, did not mean that I had to have them. I told myself I could wait until I got home to eat, and I did. I was proud of being able to curb the impulse to spend on a momentary gratification.

February 6

Today I was irritable with Gina, my assistant. This is the fourth time in two weeks, and for no good reason. I am figuring out that this book and this commitment are putting me in touch with some issues that I have long suppressed. A friend says I need to "see" someone to talk this out. I *am* seeing someone—me—and I *am* talking it out—on paper. This is therapeutic for me, this writing of the uncovering of money and food issues.

Regardless, I do not need to be irritable with Gina. I must reel in these emotions and find better ways to deal with the pain coming to the surface. It *is* painful. I don't think I really expected this to happen so I have not been prepared to deal with it. In any case, I do not need to pass the pain on to others because I am having a difficult time dealing with old memories.

Maybe more exercise will help, and I need to be sure to find ways to take good care of myself. And of course, I need to make sure I am treating Gina respectfully.

February 8

A friend and I went out to dinner at a restaurant that I have wanted to try, and my cost was $63.00. The company was good, the atmosphere pleasant, and the food was both delicious and well presented, so it was a most enjoyable evening; however, I do need to spend less on dining out.

February 9

I spoke for a group in Durham, NC, this a.m. and then boarded a plane for Los Angeles to attend a meeting with Mike. I was originally scheduled to travel with Mike to Los Angeles yesterday, but this opportunity to "make money" came up. Since 2006 is my year of financial recovery, I wisely stayed behind for a day to earn money!

Additionally, I received two calls today to speak to two different groups in late February. I planned to be out of town on personal business on those dates, which happened by coincidence to be consecutive days. I decided that I would change my personal plans to focus on business and earn money. This was an easy decision given that I am committed to my financial plan, but I am disappointed that I will miss being with Mike at a nice resort in Florida. This is an example of different decisions that I will undoubtedly need to make during this year of financial recovery.

When we are focused, the "stars line up in our favor!"

February 10-12

Mike and I spent the weekend in Los Angeles and had a great time. It was a time of relaxation for Mike; he has been working so hard and needed the time before leaving for Italy next week. I also needed the time, but mainly to catch up on time with Mike, and apparently, also to catch up on sleep. One of the best parts of the weekend was going to bed early and getting up late. Another very relaxing part was having no schedule.

My out-of-pocket expenses for the three days was $75.00. Now, that was money and time well spent!

I had a "major meltdown" on Friday, February 10th. I realized that I had a credit card payment due on the 11th, which was a Saturday. That means that it must be paid by 4:00 p.m. EST on the 10th to be on time. Unfortunately, I did not remember this until 2:00 p.m. PST, which was 5:00 p.m. EST. I called the credit card company and explained the situation. I was told that if I paid online that it would not be considered late, that it would be credited on the 11th. After a great deal of trouble trying to pay online, the online payment was made, but it showed that the payment would not be credited until the 13th.

I called the credit card company again and was told that the online payment would indeed be credited on the 13th, not the 11th, as the previous credit card company person had (erroneously) told me. Not only would my payment be late, but I had been given bad information (which is a bone of contention with me), and I had wasted over an hour of my time. Another reason I was so upset was that my interest rate on this account was already much too high and could increase because of this one late payment. There is also the likelihood of a late fee. My payment on this account is basically only paying the interest. I know this is foolish. I also know that had I not waited until the last minute to make the payment, I would not have incurred this problem. I made a decision to avoid this type of problem again on active accounts by making sure to make payments five days before they are due.

The good that came out of this is Mike and I had a discussion about paying off this card so as not to have this high interest account. The balance is less than $3000, but that interest adds up quickly. We talked about how to do this. There is always a lesson to be found in a problem.

Then there is my weight. I didn't weigh in this week, partly because I was not in town on the day that I normally weigh in and partly because I probably have gained a pound since last week and I don't want to know for sure!

I dread weighing in next week because my clothes are telling me that I have probably gained—ok, a couple of pounds. Not surprising, since I only walked twice a week for the past two weeks. I need to get back on a good eating and walking schedule before I slip back into my previous eating and exercising routines. Those routines are eating too much and exercising too little.

There really is no magic to these eating and spending plans. What I am coming to realize is that with discipline and daily focus, the weight and the spending can stay in control.

Mike and I bought Mary Grace a couple of gifts. One is for Valentine's Day. I will need to send it overnight, or it will not arrive on Valentine's Day. Again, better planning would have saved money.

The lessons I am learning include the cost of procrastinating. I know I need to do better at planning ahead, including making bill payments and mailing items. Last minute actions often cost more money and have other consequences.

Money and time are both finite. I want to learn not to spend either foolishly.

February 14

It is Valentine's Day, and my Valentine is off to Milan for an international meeting but not before bringing me a dozen red roses! We decided to do the rest of our celebrating when he returns next weekend. A friend and I went out for a light meal. Of course, we had to wait to get in since all the people who rarely go out to dinner do go to dinner on this one night. In the same vein, roses become a precious commodity, and the price doubles or triples what they cost just a few days ago. Regardless, I have to say I am delighted that Mike brought me flowers, and, without a doubt, he and I would have been in one of the packed restaurants had he not had to leave on his business trip.

I think we women are responsible for the commercial aspects of at least certain holidays, Valentine's Day being one of them. We are the ones with "expectations," not the men. Men comply, probably in part to avoid the consequences of not doing so.

I made sure I called the credit card company today about the payment delay problem and after a helpful discussion, the late fee was removed. Sometimes all we have to do is ask politely and then be persistent if that is necessary. It wasn't necessary on this occasion, I'm glad to report. I still will need to monitor the interest rate on that card. I hope the rate does not increase due to this one late payment situation.

February 16

Today was my monthly lunch bunch with a group of women business colleagues. (Yes, we refer to ourselves as the "lunch bunch.") I shared my "revolution" with them and received mixed responses. One person was quite supportive, sharing some of her own struggles. A couple of women asked good questions and seemed genuinely interested and impressed with my endeavor. A couple of others made some (perhaps) gentle chiding remarks, including how one of the decisions I gave as an example of being creative and not spending any money might be "cheating."

While I want to think that the chiding was all in jest, I am not so sure. Sometimes women have difficulty sharing another woman's success without feeling "less than." I don't want to think that today was an example of that, but it is possible. It will not detract from my resolve. In fact, it may just make my resolve stronger!

And, it will not change my desire to tell my story. There is power in sharing our own challenges and successes to help others. I am excited that a newspaper printed an article about my venture. I think that I will forward a copy to my lunch bunch and see what they have to say. Hopefully, most of them will enjoy reading it and be ready to share my journey vicariously. If one or two don't, well, that's okay too.

February 17

While getting dressed this morning, I realized that I couldn't find the jewelry that I wanted to wear because my closet was in such a mess. I decided to clean it right then and there and spent several hours going through my entire closet. This included both rearranging items so that I can find things faster and organizing my jewelry. I had a pleasant surprise by discovering a very pretty pair of earrings that I had completely forgotten about.

I set aside some clothes to donate to Goodwill, although not as many as I should have. I still have difficulty parting with things, even clothes that I haven't worn for years. I plan to work on this problem in the months ahead.

There were several boxes and bags of photos in the closet that I put aside to go through and organize when time allows.

True to my promise to myself, I paid several bills today that I normally pay later in the month. Not being so "last minute" felt good.

February 18

When I awoke this morning, those bags of clothing and boxes of photos were staring me in the face. I had planned to put them in another location and organize them later. That decision felt "heavy." I decided to work for an hour to start the process of organizing them. That at least would result in some progress. That one hour turned into three and a half. Once I got started, I made myself stay with the task, realizing that I did not have anything else any more important to do anyway. The earlier plan to go to the Antique Show and Sale seemed less important now, especially since I could not/should not buy anything that I might find there.

I decided to throw away all photo negatives and any photos that were not flattering to all people in the photo. I made piles of photos for others, including the children, Mike, and friends. Many of the photos were being saved for others anyway so why not let them decide now if they wanted to keep them? I separated photos to go into albums for the girls and Mike, and I made a promise to myself to have the albums completed in time to give them at Christmas.

Some of the "going down memory lane" was painful, such as photos taken at the time of my mother's funeral, some of the last photos of Mike's mom, and photos of my aunt and uncle, all of whom are now deceased.

February 21

I am in Florida on a business trip with Mike. This is a trip that we go on most every year. We always enjoy both the setting, wherever it might be for that year, and the group very much. This year, just as last year, my time on the trip will be abbreviated due to my speaking schedule. As a self-employed speaker and consultant, all of my income is at the pleasure of my clients. This means my clients have priority on my schedule, regardless of any personal plans unless those personal plans absolutely need my attention. Attending this business trip with Mike is a delightful personal privilege for me, but I couldn't in good conscious call it a necessity.

We arrived in Florida this morning, and I fly back to Raleigh tomorrow for those back to back speaking engagements. One's in Greensboro and one's in Research Triangle Park so the travel to and from won't be hard at all. Admittedly, I regret not being able to stay and play. But work and making money in a year of planning for financial changes need to come before personal pleasure. So they will.

This is a busy revenue week, thankfully. The first of the year got off to a slow start for me, but it is picking up significantly.

February 28th

Mary Grace will have tubes put in her ears today, and I will not be there. Tara said it was not necessary for me to be there, and, given the distance, it was too far for me to come just for that minor procedure. It is times like these that the distance between Raleigh and Georgia is especially difficult.

March 5

I worked today at the antique shop in Southport where I rent a space. I work no more than once a month there, usually on a Saturday or Sunday. My pay is $28 for five to five and a half hours, so I do not do it for the money! I like to work there occasionally to see what customers are buying. I can also work a little in my booth when we do not have customers. We just finished our annual sale. It is held every February in an attempt to bring more customers into the store since the winter months are our slowest months.

I usually enjoy being in the antique shop, but this year is different. When I am in the shop, I always see things that I want to purchase for myself or our home. I have learned that I don't have to purchase an item when I see it and that I don't have to worry that I won't find it again. Usually another one or a similar one will come along later, hopefully at a better purchasing time!

The fact that I have not yet completed the first quarter of the year of this no-spending plan, and that once I do, there are three more quarters yet to go, makes this year seem like it is stretching ahead forever.

March 12

Mary Grace turned one today! Why did her first year go so quickly while this no-spending year is going so slowly?

March 20

I had an invitation today to go on a ten-day trip to Tuscany in October of this year with a group of women. The price is reasonable, and the trip looks wonderful. Can you believe, one of my first thoughts was that I would not be able to buy anything?! One of the excursions is to a place that has many designer items, including Prada. I immediately started thinking of reasons that I should delay this trip with the main reason being my commitment to limited spending.

Then I thought, who knows if I will have another opportunity to make this trip? After all, we aren't promised tomorrow. I have a dilemma. Do I take advantage of this wonderful travel opportunity and stick to my commitment not to spend except for gifts for others, or do I delay the trip until I can spend freely?

This decision is my greatest challenge since this spending, or better said, not spending, plan went into effect. I have not been seriously tempted, or at least not tempted much, since the start of my journey. This is definitely a test! First, I recognize how very fortunate I am to have the opportunity and the resources to be able to make the trip. That part does not change the challenge I have set for myself. I want to be able to keep my commitment, and I am afraid that the temptation to spend on non-allowable items will be too great to do so.

What shall I do? I am not sure of the best decision for me.

March 21

I decided to try to go to Tuscany if a condition is met. The trip is most cost effective if two women share a room, so going with a friend would make the trip more affordable as well as more fun. I have two friends in mind who might be interested in the trip. Either of these women would be a good traveling companion.

If either of these women can go, then I will try to go. If neither friend can go that will be my sign to skip this trip this year.

I am anxious to know the outcome of this "condition experiment."

March 24

"There's a lot you can do without money when you are not focused on needing money." I heard this quote on NPR today and decided to modify it to be my mantra this year. I changed the quote to "There is a lot you can do without things when you are not focused on needing things."

March 29

I am learning how to slow down and not be so impulsive in my spending. In the past, I would have bought many things this year, especially clothes, although I am not a "clothes horse."

Instead, I am spending more time in my closet than I normally do, deciding what clothes to wear from those that I have.

Well, it isn't true that I only have a few clothes. What *is* true is that I wear some clothes over and over and rarely wear others at all. My closet is full of clothing I have bought on impulse. Some still have tags on them years later! Why am I not able to get rid of those clothes that I obviously will never wear? Is it because I bought them and do not want to admit that I made a mistake in buying them? Or is it because I think that I will wear them at some point? What is the statute of limitations on clothes purchased and never worn?

I have an Anne Klein silk jacket that I have never worn. I bought it at least fifteen years ago. It did not look good on me when I bought it. I try it on at least once a year, realize that it still doesn't look good on me, and then I put it back in the closet. Why I put it back in the closet, I do not know. If it did not look good on me when I bought it and doesn't look good on me when I try it on yearly, do I think that it will suddenly become attractive on me? I need to tell myself to be realistic. Instead, I must be telling myself that miracles will happen with this jacket, and it will all of a sudden become attractive on me! The question, I wonder, is when do I think that will happen?

March 31

Well, I made it through the first quarter of this spending recovery plan, hallelujah! I am proud of that fact and remain convinced that I can and will stay committed for the entire year.

Just as I expected, though, it is getting harder. Spring is here, and I would love to buy some new clothes. Also, I do need shoes, although I have many pairs in my closet. Most of my shoes I never wear, just like many, and maybe most, of my clothes. When I say that I *need* shoes at this point, it is quite true. I have worn holes in my most casual pair because I wear them so often. I need new walking shoes too. I only have one pair of walking shoes, and that pair is getting so worn that they are painful to wear. That is not a good health thing.

So here is the dilemma. I walk at least three days a week, and usually four or five days, as part of my fitness and health regimen. It is important to have walking shoes that fit properly to be able to walk, and these walking shoes no longer qualify. Mike bought me a pair of walking shoes earlier in the year as a gift, but the sole is coming apart on them. Since he purchased them at a company store in another state, returning them for a new pair would not be easy.

I don't think that I can justify buying new walking shoes when I have a pair that needs to be replaced by the manufacturer, even if to do so takes more time and is not as convenient. I am realizing that saving money often requires taking more time. Time and money are often a trade-off. (My mind digressed and flashed on the example of convenience foods. Convenience foods cost more than "non convenience... or inconvenient?" foods, in large part because they are easier and quicker to prepare, but they are probably not as healthy for us.)

Okay, I'm back from the digression. The decision about the walking shoes is clear. I will not purchase the shoes.

First Quarter

Challenges and Insights

January 1, 2017

Rereading this journal ten years later brings some different perspectives. I have refused to allow myself to change the content, although I wanted to at times—especially in a couple of places. One of those places was in the first quarter mention of my mother.

I understand more clearly now that while my mother did not provide the nurturing relationship I wanted and needed, she did the very best that she could. My mother lived an unhappy life for most of her years. If I had faced the struggles she did, I probably would not have done as well.

Her story was quite a sad one. Her father was an alcoholic. He was also abusive, although I do not know to what degree or whom he abused other than my grandmother.

When my mother was fourteen, she was raped. This was in the 1940s, a very different social time than now. The man was tried for the crime and went to prison. The crime against my mother was very public knowledge. Her attacker was a black man. The intolerance of society then proved even harsher because of that. She was shamed and ostracized. She quit school before graduating.

Her life continued to be complicated. She became pregnant when she was 17 and married my legal father, a man she lived with only a short time. Mother never discussed my paternal situation with me, but others did.

For many years, my mother was a functioning alcoholic, and we had a troubled relationship. Thankfully, we repaired our relationship, and, for the last few years before she died, we were closer, although not as close as I wish we could have been.

To this day, I grieve that I did not show my mother more of my love or do for her what I could have done had I not been self-righteous and consumed with "things." While I would like to "clean up" up the self-righteous parts in the journal, I will not allow myself to do so. It was what I was thinking and feeling at the time, so I am showing "warts" and all.

Mother went to her grave in 1998 at the age of 64, shamed again. This time it was by her third husband, a man she loved who left her for another woman.

Looking back on those years, it is clear to me that my mother was a stronger woman than I credited her. If she had not had some strength, the events of her life surely would have broken her completely. I have led a privileged life in comparison. Shame on me for focusing on the TV dinners, failing to recognize at the time that she put food on the table for me, that she gave me life when she could have chosen not to, and that she loved me and showed me so in the only ways that she could.

In the first section of the journal, the recognition of the importance of food and the connection of that to the way I spent money felt dramatic to me. I was trying to nurture myself as an adult with "things" and food, not understanding at that point that external things never satisfy what the heart and soul lack.

Because food was such a focus for me, struggling with weight problems was, and is, a natural by-product. I am once again needing to lose twenty pounds, the same twenty pounds I have gained and lost many times through the years. I begin again today.

Second Quarter 2006

April 17

Easter Sunday was yesterday. Mike, Chatham, and I spent it in Douglasville with Tara, Stephen, and Mary Grace. Mary Grace is thirteen months old, and soon she will be walking. In fact, she walked several steps three different times this weekend, her first tentative attempts. She is taking her time with the walking, maybe realizing that once you begin to be independent, there is no turning back.

Well, that isn't true, either part of it. That a thirteen-month-old can reason to that degree is obviously untrue. The statement that once you begin to be independent, there is no turning back is not true either. I have been independent several times in my fifty-four years, but I did "turn back." I experienced dependency, especially in one particular area, for too many years recently.

My first memory of being independent was when I went to college. My college education was paid for with grants and loans. I had no family financial assistance, or family assistance at all, for that matter. I was eighteen at the time and went to college already engaged to be married to a man four years my senior. We married after my first year of college, and he relocated from Alabama to Virginia while I continued through college.

We lived in an apartment, and he worked at a radio station. I went on through my college experience at the normal rate, graduating in four years with a nursing degree. I don't remember much about those years, especially related to finances. My memory tells me that we were the usual "less than prosperous" young couple, with average material possessions. I remember we made a bookcase of cinderblocks and wood and that it was actually attractive.

I don't remember anything else about our "stuff." My guess is that we didn't have much. I do know that I did not feel "poor." I knew very well how poor felt, having lived with my maternal grandmother for many of my younger years. I watched her struggle financially, getting by some months with government assistance, such as commodity cheese. I did not feel poor then either, although we obviously were. As I think about that now, I wonder if my grandmother's love sheltered me from any feelings of poverty. My most vivid memories of that time are not related to money or material possessions, but of family and love.

The marriage I entered at nineteen lasted a little less than ten years, ending in divorce. During those years I went through many changes. Although in hindsight, I realize that I outgrew the man and the marriage long before it ended, the fact that it ended did not have as much to do with me as it did with him. I thought that I was happy with him, and even if I wasn't, marriage is forever, isn't it? If you make your bed, don't you lie in it? I realize now that I had no basis for comparison. I only knew of a few couples, all in my paternal grandparents' church, who had what seemed like a good marriage. My views of family life were vastly skewed.

My commitment to our marriage was not enough to sustain it. For a marriage to work, commitment is required by both partners, and no one else can be involved to change the commitment. After separating a couple of times toward the end, a divorce was the obvious, yet painful, decision. There wasn't enough between us to sustain us.

Since I am so prone to hang onto things, I am somewhat surprised that I did not stay in that first marriage, thinking I could "fix it." After all, I am a person of commitment, and once made, commitments aren't to be broken, or so I thought at that time in my life. I learned from that experience that both people in a relationship must be committed. My commitment to that marriage shifted to my commitment to my sanity and our daughter. To this day, even though Mike and I are happily married, I grieve that Tara and Chatham are children of divorce.

This time after the divorce is the second time that I remember being truly independent, and in being independent, finding a self that not only could manage on my own but also could be responsible for someone else, my daughter. That was in 1980, a time when many women in similar circumstances made different choices. I do not need to judge their choices; all I am accountable for are mine.

As I think about this, I need to differentiate clearly between financial independence and emotional independence. I have usually been emotionally independent but not always financially independent. My first marriage was a time that I was not emotionally independent. Looking back on that marriage choice years later, I realized that I married to have a home and a family more than to have a husband. He had a wonderful family, and, in hindsight, I realize that I needed a family and a home of my own. What does a nineteen-year-old coming from the type of family system in which I was reared know about marriage? The answer is clear. Nothing!

There must be some lessons in my history as to when I have been most and least financially independent. I want to figure this out. Independence in women has long been an interest of mine. In fact, in a graduate program in Sociology in the mid-1980s, my research question related to this issue. I did not continue in that program or the research, but the research question still intrigues me, more on a personal level now than on a professional level.

What is the relationship in my life between financial independence and emotional independence? Is it true that I have usually been emotionally independent? What does that even mean? I can think of times in my life other than the first marriage that I have hung on to a breaking rope in the spirit of commitment, not letting go until the rope was broken and pulled from me. Another of those times was when I held onto a job that was slipping away from me, not letting go until I was fired. In both of those situations, the broken marriage and the broken job, I could not, would not, quit. Is that because I was too emotionally committed, and if so, why? I think my sense of self was too tied up in both of those "positions" to let go. I will try to figure this out more as I go through this year of financial recovery. Surely the answers are in this mess somewhere.

April 22

Amazing. Mike and I are en route to Las Vegas, connecting through Atlanta. At the departure gate in Atlanta, we ran into Troy, husband number one, the one I wrote about earlier! Who "woulda thunk it"? Of all of the people in the world, all the places one can travel, what is the likelihood that two people from a previous marriage would meet in a different state than either of them lives, both traveling to another state, many miles away? This life of ours is really interesting! Elisabeth Kubler-Ross writes in her book, *The Wheel of Life*, that there are no accidents, that all things happen for a reason, even if we cannot figure out the "why" at the time. If I believe this as I have said that I do, what is the lesson in this? What could be the reason for this chance airport meeting?

I am so thankful that husband number one and I have come to a place of comfort for those times when it is necessary that we, now "outlaws," are together. All of those times are centered on Tara and Mary Grace. The fact that we can be together without the animosity makes it so much easier for everyone, especially Tara. Hopefully, Mary Grace will never know the discomfort. While it isn't "totally natural," it is usually fairly comfortable. I have worked hard for this, and most others have as well. I wish the same were true for Mike's "first." One of the differences is that there have not yet been many occasions for all of Chatham's family to *need* to be together. Chatham has not married and has no children, so we are not "thrown together" in those situations.

Thank goodness for one thing. Mike and I and husband number one are all seated in coach. Silly or not, I would not want to be in coach and see husband number one in first! I guess that has something to do with "stuff."

April 23

I am in Las Vegas, walking the strip, with three other women. I came for the socializing, as well as to see the area since this is my first time in Las Vegas. I had not expected the city, or more accurately said, the hotels, to be so beautiful. The other women shopped, although they looked more than they purchased. I was not tempted to buy. I was so happy just taking in the beauty of my surroundings.

We spent most of our time at the Venetian. We went to the Canyon Ranch Spa there and inquired about the different treatments and packages. I had called ahead for their information since I had been to the Canyon Ranch resort in Tucson. The prices are high, but the facility is beautiful. We all decided to come back another day to enjoy our selected treatments since we were not prepared today. After visiting the spa, we enjoyed a lovely, light lunch.

April 24

I went to the program this morning in Las Vegas and did not see the friends that I went to the strip with yesterday. We did not make firm plans for our spa treatments and ended up not getting together. At dinner that evening I learned that one of the women had decided to go to the spa at our hotel. I still plan to get at least a pedicure and probably a massage at Canyon Ranch although I have not decided when. I want to make sure I get my walk in first. I do not want to ruin a pedicure by walking. Also, I want to be sure that this is how I want to spend money. I decided that I would work on my impulsiveness and wait to decide about the spa treatments. I have several more days here. I want to plan well what I do, especially related to spending money.

April 25

I had one of my hardest issues today related to not spending. In the Forum shops at Caesar's Palace, there is a Taryn Rose shop. I have long admired Taryn Rose shoes and would have bought a pair a couple of different times (before this year, of course!) if I had been able to find them in my size. I did not know that there were Taryn Rose shops; I had found the shoes in a department store. They are expensive shoes. I have never paid that amount of money for one pair of shoes. While they are expensive, they are worth it due to the way that they are made. Taryn Rose is an orthopedic surgeon, and her shoes are good for the feet, as well as beautiful. Since I am on my feet a lot and need to be dressed professionally, I do not question the value. But this is a different year, and I am not supposed to buy shoes this year. I struggled with this decision not to buy the shoes for two reasons: the sales person offered me a discount since the only pair in my size was the display pair, and he also said he would waive the sales tax since I live out of state.

I struggled with the Taryn Rose shoe issue. Remember, when I started this plan in January part of my plan was that I could purchase necessary business items, including clothes and shoes, if I really needed them. I almost convinced myself that I needed those shoes, not because I didn't have any shoes for business, but because they would be better for my feet. After thinking this through for what seemed like forever, I decided to leave the store and walk around and ponder my options. The salesperson gave me a card, offering to honor the same terms if I decided to purchase them after returning home. That took the immediate heat off of my decision. I still decided to walk around that mall and determine the right thing to do in this situation.

I left the mall after about an hour, having convinced myself to return home without the shoes, inventory my business shoes, and decide if I still thought that I needed them and should not wait until this year is over. If I decided I needed them at that point, then I would order the shoes.

I believe that I conquered something major for me with this decision.

April 26

I walked four hours today through the Las Vegas strip and was amazed at all of the things there were to purchase. I did make a purchase today. Mike and I will celebrate our 22nd anniversary on Friday. I had not decided what to get him. When I found some beautiful Italian neckties and they were on sale, I knew I had found my anniversary gift to Mike. I happily purchased the gift for him and managed to ignore the beautiful leather purses.

Several times since the beginning of the year (and the plan), I have thought about things that I want for our home. I had wondered if it was consistent with the plan to ask Mike for any of those for our anniversary. I thought that while I have done that in past years, it would not be appropriate this year. If Mike decided to give me a gift for the house and it truly was his idea, that would be different and acceptable. That would be a real gift. My usual "naming of what I want for occasions" doesn't result in a gift at all but is a fulfillment of a request.

April 28

For our anniversary, Mike gave me beautiful 18-carat gold earrings from Italy as well as a trip to Italy in October! The trip to Italy is the one that I mentioned several weeks ago. I was torn as to whether to go, knowing that Tuscany is a wonderful area for shopping and I would need to stick to my no (unallowed) spending commitment. Since I was so torn about whether to go on this trip, I made the "condition" with myself that I would go if one of my friends could go with me. Brenda wants to go! Interestingly enough, Brenda and her husband Bruce were the couple with us in New Orleans at the time I made this year-of-no-spending commitment. Synchronicity? The trip will be enjoyable without spending, and with Mike's gift of the trip (which he said is for not just our anniversary, but also my birthday and Christmas!), I decided to go. I am really excited about it.

I am not so sure that the two neckties that I gave Mike for our anniversary compare favorably at all to his gifts to me. I am struck by the fact that the neckties I bought Mike are Italian. That was not planned. But then, synchronicity never is.

May 5

Mike and I are in Myrtle Beach for the weekend. I am speaking tonight at a conference. I thought about getting a pedicure at the resort spa. The cost of a pedicure (allowed spending) at this resort is more than double the cost at home. I checked times available for tomorrow but did not make an appointment. I want to think about whether to spend that much money on a pedicure. It's hard to believe the pedicure here will be twice as good as one at home.

You may be wondering why a pedicure is an allowed expense. Pedicures and manicures are in the category of services, not tangible items. I decided at the beginning of this plan that services would be allowed. While they are allowed spending, I do want them to be reasonable expenses, not excessive ones.

May 6

A phone call from our youngest daughter Chatham's boyfriend changed our schedule for the day. The call was a request for Mike's blessing for them to get married. We were caught totally off guard although we probably should not have been. We knew that their relationship was getting serious. Chatham is soon to be 29, so she is certainly old enough to marry without needing our blessing, although we appreciate being included in their decision.

Mike's answer to the "blessing" question was that he would not have that conversation on the phone. He offered to meet in person once back in Raleigh (the town where we all live) the first of the week. Before meeting with the "groom to be," Mike planned to meet with "the bride to be." After all, this is the 21st century, and our daughter is not property to be delivered from her father to a husband. It is important to us not just to give our blessing to the union but to feel comfortable that we, her father especially, have discussed this fully with her. We are not sure that Chatham is ready to marry, even at 29.

So much for the pedicure. Mike and I just needed to be with each other and talk. Marriage is serious business, especially when it involves one of our children!

May 10

This has been a busy week, especially for Mike. In addition to his normal work schedule, including getting ready for a two-week trip out of the country, Mike had individual conversations with the soon-to-be-engaged couple. We agreed that it was best for me to let him handle this alone. There have been only a few times in our marriage of twenty-two years that we have decided to "divide" our time with our children. If you are doing the math, you may have figured out that our youngest daughter isn't mine biologically. She became my daughter when Mike and I married. He had custody of Chatham, who was six years old at that time and from his first marriage, and I had custody of Tara, who was eight years old and from my first marriage. We never used the word "step," although both daughters have other parents. "Step" just did not seem to fit for our family. Even so, there have been a few times that we have decided that I take the lead with Tara and he with Chatham. We decided that this was one of those times.

After those intense discussions with the bride and groom to be, Mike left on his business trip to Germany, Holland, and India. We did not know what the engagement plans would be, although it was clear that an engagement would be forthcoming at some point.

May 28

There has been so much emotion regarding our youngest daughter the last couple of weeks. She will marry next summer. After all of the discussions, we, of course, gave them our blessing. We hope this marriage will be right for both of them. Mike and I both have had marriages that did not work out, so we are clearly not experts on this issue.

In times past, one way that I dealt with stress was to lose myself in shopping. I did not always know that was what I was doing, but I can see now that it was. Another coping mechanism in my life has been eating. I am no longer doing emotional eating or emotional spending. I am struck by the fact that I am getting both weaknesses under control at the same time, and hopefully, once and for all. In my case, it seems to be true that making one important change makes it easier to make others.

I have lost and gained the same ten to twenty pounds for most of my adult life. The last time I lost twenty pounds was a few months before our oldest daughter Tara's wedding in 2002. I regained the weight gradually. In January 2005, I took myself back to Weight Watchers to once again lose the weight. At the time, I wasn't fully committed to the weight loss. In sixteen months, I have only lost fourteen pounds. I am proud of the fact that I have lost those pounds, but it is clear to me now that had I been truly committed, I would have lost more weight more quickly.

Since becoming committed to this no-spending plan, I have also become committed to my weight loss plan. In the past month, I have noticed a difference in my behavior in this regard, and I think it is related to the cementing of resolve about spending. More than about spending or eating, this is really about control, being in control, and not letting bad choices control me.

There are other changes that I need to make in both spending and eating, but I do need to acknowledge my successes also. I like the person that I am becoming. Taking this year to get in control of my spending habit is making my journey of getting in control of my eating also more successful.

The important word is "control." Focus and discipline are necessary aspects of getting and staying in control. Counting daily, whether it is counting Weight Watchers points or counting dollars, helps keep me in control. If a few days go by and I have not counted food points, I can count on the fact that I have had more food points than I would have believed. The same is true for money. If I do not balance my checkbook routinely and stay within my budget, I am shocked at what I have spent, even on "allowed" purchases.

The same is true for writing. While taking the recent two-week break from journaling the journey may be understandable, I can feel the difference when I write. The act of writing today has made me feel much more connected to my important lessons. The connection of the spending plan and the eating plan is insight that I have from today's journaling. Granted, I have had some thoughts of this previously, but I had not made the connection in the same way as I do now.

And to be honest, while I have counted my points this past couple of weeks and I have continued to lose weight, I have not been counting my money and staying on top of my spending. While I have not slipped and purchased any non-allowable items for myself or the house, I have probably spent more on allowable purchases than necessary. By saying "I have probably," I am admitting that I do not know because I have not recorded and monitored my spending! That will change today. Denial is never as powerful as knowledge, especially when that knowledge is coupled with creative ways to resolve the need for new items.

An example of a creative way to handle a need is in the area of my lipstick. Now lipstick is an allowable purchase when it is a replacement and when I do not have any other tubes of lipstick of that same or similar color. I need to replace two different colors of lipstick. Unfortunately, one of those colors has been discontinued by the manufacturer. The other I have not been able to locate. My creative solution is to use a lipstick brush, which I already had. I do not like to use the lipstick brush because it takes longer to apply my lipstick. Regardless of the fact that it takes a little more time, I can use both lipsticks longer by using a brush than is possible without this type of application. This is obviously a money-saving benefit, and maybe even more important for me, it is also possible for me to use my preferred colors longer.

Perhaps you are thinking that my example is so trite. Maybe so, but if I save in several small ways, those add up to bigger savings. I am also conserving resources, including time and products as well as money. The time taken to use the lipstick brush saves travel time and gas going to the mall, not to mention I don't have to make a purchase at this point.

June 30

If you are noticing the dates of my entries, you should immediately find the "disconnect" in what I wrote last about journaling. I have not written anything in over a month. And if you reread the previous section, it will be as clear to you as it is to me that I haven't kept my commitment to myself after all! This reality reinforces how hard it is for me to stay focused. I am great at starting things, not nearly as good at "staying the course."

I am still on the "no non-allowed spending part of the plan." I am proud of that. I do need to stay disciplined, however, about those other things in the plan, such as writing in this journal at least once a week, staying within my budget, and counting food points.

What has been going on with me these last four weeks? What are the variables that have affected my choices not to write, manage my money well, or manage my weight well? I know intellectually that those positive behaviors make a profound difference in my success, so why do I continue to make the same mistakes or make the same choices?

Well, Mary Grace was with us for a week, and what a joyful, yet hectic time that was! We forget what energy and time small children require. I am still recovering, yet ready to have her again. That isn't a good reason for not being able to write at all that week. Many writers with families manage to get their writing done, so I really should not use Mary Grace's visit with us as an excuse for not writing.

Also, Mike and I were on a week-long international trip to Greece and Romania. It was not easy to find time to write due to planned events. But then, those are just excuses, not reasons. And with life being what it is, there will always be times that it is easier, or more difficult, to keep certain priorities just that, priorities. I must find a way to keep my promises to myself during the times when it is not easy to do. Especially then because those are the very times that I need to do so the most.

Second Quarter

Challenges and Insights

January 1, 2017

Reading the journal entries from the second quarter of 2006, I see the same old struggles—money and food. These have been lifelong challenges for me.

While I was successful in staying with my commitment of no personal spending during this quarter, my "commitment" to journal the journey weekly, or even every other week, fell by the wayside. The two main reasons for this were travel and major life events, both distracting me from staying focused.

I have been open about the fact that I am good at starting things but not as good at finishing them. I also struggle with staying focused. These traits resulted in me not writing on the schedule that I promised myself—or even writing regularly. While I knew that writing regularly was important for me on several levels (accountability, staying focused, and gaining insights), it still was easy for me to veer off course. I failed to budget my money, which I feel contributed to me failing to count my calories/Weight Watcher points. I was again on the yoyo of gaining a pound and losing a pound, or some combination of gaining and losing.

The importance to me of relationships, especially with family, is a continuing theme in the second quarter's writings. Times with Mike and Mary Grace nurtured in a way that food couldn't. Travel with Mike was satisfying more because we were together than any of the other benefits travel provided. This is even more true today.

And Mary Grace was growing and changing so much during that year that I wanted to be with her as much as possible. Now, in 2017, there is ten-year-old Elsie and four-year-old Virginia in addition to twelve-year-old Mary Grace. Times with them and the rest of our family remain a major priority for me. So while travel and concentrated times with family did distract from my writing during that year, I would not trade any of those times with family for more writing time.

Our youngest daughter's decision to marry and our involvement in that decision also distracted my attention from my writing commitment. Chatham and Johnathan did marry in 2007 and are still married. They have chosen not to have children, but they spend as much time as they can nurturing their nieces.

The importance to me of beauty is reflected in the second quarter's writings. Beauty is not a "want" for me; it is a need. I connected to this fact when I did some life planning after losing my job in the early 1990s. At that time, a good friend of mine, Kathleen Harwell, coordinated several life planning sessions with me and another friend. While I do not remember the specific activity we did that made this connection in me, that insight was dramatic at the time and has been reinforced in many ways in the subsequent years.

As I read the section on Las Vegas, I could re-live the beauty of the area and the hotels, remembering all that more than the casinos or the wealth of things to buy in the shops. Beauty is not always expensive—the beauty found in nature is even free. However, many things that are beautiful are expensive. I know that my need for beauty, and its cousin quality, result in me purchasing some things that I cannot really afford. I also know, however, that although I have many clothes, I only wear those that are made well with a certain level of quality and beauty, such as St. John suits. When I do the cost/benefit analysis, I realize that the actual cost per wear of my St. John items makes them more affordable than some other items in my closet. And they are timeless. So, one insight I gained is that it is more economical to own fewer items and make them ones that are beautiful and of good quality. So, no Fast Fashion for me!

Third Quarter 2006

July 12

Again, I have not written for two weeks. Am I now on a twice a month writing schedule instead of a weekly writing schedule? It seems so.

I arrived at Las Vegas Lakes today at 12:30 a.m., but my luggage didn't. I am speaking here for a national association. Thankfully, my speech is tomorrow. If necessary, I can speak in what I wore on the plane although I would prefer to wear something I have not traveled in. I wore pants and a jacket, so I will be presentable if my luggage does not arrive. I may be able to buy something to wear in the hotel shops, but I doubt that I will be able to find dressier clothes to buy off the rack. I am short and usually have to have pants altered. At the moment, I do not know what I will do about this dilemma.

On the one hand, this is a legitimate reason to buy some new clothes. I am seven months into my no-spending plan, and it is getting rather tiresome. Now I have a legitimate reason to shop for new clothes! On the other hand, I do not want to buy anything new. I do want to go this entire year wearing what I have and not purchasing anything new. I want to prove to myself that I can do it.

I am recovering from a bad cold, so I think that I will stay in the hotel and rest. The room includes a robe, so I am fine, at least for a few hours. I hung up my clothes that I wore on the plane. I'm saving them for tomorrow, just in case. The airlines gave me a vanity pack with a toothbrush and other toiletries. I will wait until late afternoon for my luggage to arrive before deciding whether to purchase any clothes. If necessary, I can go to the hotel gift shop and buy some resort logo wear. But I think that I will wait awhile before doing anything. The resort robe is quite comfortable.

July 13

I made it! My luggage arrived yesterday about 4 p.m. I stuck to my decision and waited, so I did not make any clothes purchases. I am so proud of myself. That was a real test, and I passed it.

Coincidentally, I read in today's paper about a woman who wore the same brown dress for an entire year. If she could do *that*, I can do *this*!

July 14

I arrived in New York this morning. Thankfully, my suitcase also arrived. Unfortunately, my best pair of dress shoes may be ruined. Something, I think it was hairspray, leaked on them. I now have to decide if I will buy a new pair. There is a much better selection here than at home. You may remember that clothes and shoes for business are allowable purchases on my plan, but only if necessary.

I think that I will wait and try to resist making a shoe purchase.

I have learned these last few days that by waiting, I was able to avoid making a purchase. I do have other dress shoes at home, although none as good for some outfits. But I will wait. Perhaps I can make do with these. It is at least worth a try.

July 16

I have worn the same black capris for three days. Although I have a suitcase full of clothes, my black capris are so comfortable that I have worn them three days in a row, each day with a different top. Perhaps because my husband is the only one I know here, and he doesn't care what I wear, I can allow myself to do this. But even though they are comfortable and Mike does not mind seeing me in them several consecutive days, they are beginning to look worn.

My favorite black dress jacket is also looking like it needs to be retired. The lining is frayed, so much so that the threads have had to be clipped. I wonder if I should get the lining replaced. No, that will not be done. The jacket is also looking "shiny." It needs to be retired. But I do not know what to wear in its place. This no-spending plan makes me not want to buy another one, even if I can find another one I like as well. Perhaps this jacket will last another month or two, which will involve wearing it no more often than perhaps once a week during that time. Then it will be fall, and other clothes can be worn. The fact that the seasons change has helped with this plan. Thank goodness clothes can be rotated seasonally, resulting in longer wear and some much-desired variety.

But what of the woman with the brown dress? I guess she did not worry about tiring of wearing the same thing every day since she wore the brown dress 365 days in a row. Wow.

July 20

I had coffee today with a client and wanted to wear closed-toed dress shoes. I am doing a session for her staff soon on professional dress, so it was important to be sure to dress for that image. Unfortunately, my best closed-toed dress shoes are the ones that something leaked on recently in my suitcase. I assumed at the time they were ruined, but once they dried and after trying them on, I decided that they could be saved.

Before this year's plan, I most likely would have thrown out those shoes and bought another pair. This might still be necessary, but not without trying to make these shoes last.

July 21

You may be wondering how I am doing with my budget and weight management plan. Well, not so well on either. To be totally honest, although I have not been spending much, I haven't done my budgeting. As for my weight, it creeps up two to three pounds when I am not diligently counting points, and I haven't been lately.

How many promises do I plan to break to myself until I get serious about both of these areas of money and weight? At different times in my life, I have found all of the forces to be with me once I made a commitment and kept it. The opposite is also true. In my first book, *How to Thrive in Spite of Mess, Stress and Less!*, I made a promise that I clearly have not kept: to get and stay in control of my weight and my finances. I even wrote, "By the time that you read this, I will have my weight and finances in control." Well, it occurs to me that since I have not kept that promise, the books have not sold as I envisioned they would. There may be a connection there. Promises are serious business.

Do not make a promise that you do not keep, not even, or maybe especially, to yourself.

July 28

My weight is still such a struggle. Once again being "down to the wire" with needing to weigh in at Weight Watchers, and not wanting to see the two-pound weight gain on my record, I realize that this is a game. The game I am playing is planning to lose these two pounds by the end of the month. When and where to weigh in this month is a challenge. Weighing in must be no later than Monday, July 31st since that is the last day of the month. To remain in good standing with WW, I have to weigh in at least once a month. Well, not surprisingly (to me, at least), I have not weighed in this month. And I will be out of town on Monday. Mike and I are going to be in Douglasville, GA, for the weekend to celebrate our son-in-law Stephen's thirtieth birthday. I will stay for a couple of days and visit family in surrounding areas. On Monday, I will be with a dear friend who is undergoing surgery that day in Gadsden, AL, and will then spend the night with another dear friend in another city in Alabama. I have not figured out how or where to weigh in on Monday, which is the last day of the month. One option is to skip weighing in this month and start over with WW. I do not want to do that, but at this point, I do not know if I can work it out any other way.

I should remember this as a great example of waiting to the last minute, something that I do too often in various ways. Why put such stress on myself? Do I enjoy living on the edge like this? There is a school of thought that says yes, that someone with my personality does just that.

As bothered by myself as I am right now, I need to think of the positive. At least I am focused on my weight and am trying to find a way to stay in balance with it. Those two to three pounds that seem to creep back too often will come off and stay off if/when I consistently do those things that need to be done. Knowing what to do is not a mystery. Doing it is the hard part. Looking on the bright side, at least this time it isn't five pounds, or more, that has once again crept back. Apparently I am better with this than I used to be, although I am not where I want to be.

One step forward, two steps back. It would be better if it could be two steps forward, one step back!

July 30

I went to the mall in Douglasville, GA, today to buy nail polish. My polish is chipped, and money plan notwithstanding, I will not be seen in public with chipped nail polish. I went to Dillard's department store because I have two $25 gift cards, and I decided to use one of those for the purchase. I have considered whether I should use the gift cards or not. I received them as Christmas gifts, so I think it is reasonable that I can use them to buy anything that I want since the purchase would be a gift and would not be using my money to purchase something. Also, nail polish is an allowable expense, with or without the gift cards. One aspect of being "polished" professionally is to have manicured nails, although one does not have to have colored nail polish to look professional.

Should I use money instead of gift cards for the nail polish purchase so that I can buy a "non-allowed" item with the gift cards? No, I do not want to do that; it is not technically acceptable.

So there I was at the mall ready to make an allowable purchase, and I had decided to use the gift cards instead of money, a decision of which I was proud. Unfortunately, I could not find any nail polish in a color that I will wear. I went to every make-up counter in several department stores, and I was amazed at the lack of color selection. It seems that all of the cosmetic lines are eliminating nail polish. I wonder if that has to do with the major increase in people having manicures and pedicures in salons instead of doing their own nails. I do not know how long this has been the case since it has been quite a while (probably a couple of years) since I have purchased polish.

I had no choice but to go to a nail salon and have a manicure and pedicure. In my professional work, I cannot have chipped polish. So instead of using a gift card for a purchase that would probably have cost no more than ten dollars, I spent thirty-eight dollars (including gratuity) for a manicure and pedicure. That was a good price and, as a service, an allowable expense.

Although I am okay with the outcome of the decision I had to make, it is somewhat deflating to lose the option of how I wanted to make this decision! On the other hand, I still have my Dillard's gift cards to use on something else!

August 4

Mike bought me new walking shoes today. New Balance had a sale, and it was also a tax-free weekend. We decided that my feet should not suffer any longer in the old shoes. These new shoes became a necessity. If I am going to continue to walk for exercise and health, then it makes no sense for me to walk in shoes that hurt my feet. I had decided that I was going to have to buy the shoes myself soon. This would have been the only thing that I would have purchased for myself in eight months. It is good that I did not have to buy them. Not so much because of the money, but because of the plan. I do not want to break this promise to myself. On the other hand, I do not want to be foolish either and wear shoes that are bad for my feet. It is becoming easier for me to differentiate wants from needs.

On the other hand, are the shoes really a need? I know there are people who can't afford to buy new shoes, even when their feet need them. There are many children in the world who do not even have shoes. The fact that my feet get new shoes when they "need" them may be more of a luxury than a necessity. In some countries, even in some areas in my own city, what is considered a necessity to some is not even an available option to others.

Still, I do see shoes that fit well more a necessity than a "want" and wish we all had shoes.

August 6

What is it about my shoes? They all seem to be wearing out. My favorite casual shoes are falling apart. Both shoes have split to the point that I cannot wear them.

My favorite business casual dress shoes are also showing signs of wear. They are black patent leather, and I wear them several times a week. They are looking worn, although that is hopefully not visible to anyone else! The problem is the patent leather is coming off at the toe area. These shoes remind me of the black jacket that has the worn lining that hopefully only I can see.

Thankfully I still have other shoes that I can wear, although none that I like as well as these two pairs. I suppose that is just, "oh well."

August 16

I am off to Denver to meet with a branding expert to work on my business brand. I met this individual at the recent National Speakers Association convention and decided that it is time for me to focus on my brand. I think he is the one who can help me. It isn't inexpensive. I hope it will be worth it. How is one to know? There are no guarantees. I do believe branding is important so hopefully this will be a good investment.

August 20

The trip to Denver was good. I came back with a new business brand. At least I think I did. I need to let it "jell." This move is something that I think is a good decision, but I do not want to be impulsive about this. Building a new brand is very expensive if it is integrated into all aspects of one's business. There is no urgency other than if I wait, someone else may create a similar and potentially competitive brand identity.

August 25

We are off to Sint Maarten/Saint Martin for two wonderful weeks! I have packed mainly very casual clothes. As I pack, I realize that some of these clothes are really showing their wear and this is probably the last time that some of them will be worn. I have packed three pairs of Fresh Produce cotton knit pants that will not see another summer. One pair has a small hole in the leg, and the two others have permanent spots. Although the hole and the spots are not that obvious, I will not wear them out of the house at home. But in the very casual islands, I can wear them without worry. I will miss these pants since they are so comfortable. I have missed not being able to purchase Fresh Produce apparel this year. I love the brand! Their clothes are so colorful and comfortable, and they are the perfect beachwear. I look forward to being able to replace my supply next spring.

I do believe that I will be a much more discriminating shopper after this year of a different spending plan and that what I purchase will not be impulse buys. It is clear that although I have a closet full of clothes, there are some clothes that seem to get worn much more often than others. The same is true for jewelry. Some of my jewelry has not been worn in years and probably will not ever be worn again. Yet, how can I part with it? That is so difficult. It makes sense to go through the jewelry and take out the pieces that have not been worn and probably will not be. I can offer them to the girls, put some aside for Mary Grace and our yet to be born grandchild (if it is a girl, which we will know tomorrow!), and sell the rest.

Why not do that? What good is that jewelry doing since it gets "lost" in the drawers and just collects dust? If a piece hasn't been worn in more than a year, how likely is it that it will ever be worn again?

The obvious answer is, not likely at all.

But it is still not so obvious that I will be able to part with those items—for emotional reasons, not practical ones. I have a hard time letting go of anything.

Maybe I will be better able to deal with these issues at the end of this year.

September 9

We left St. Maarten today, but not before going shopping one last time. Our shopping today was souvenir shopping. Our only purchases were two coffee mugs, a spoon rest, and a tea bag holder. Mike made these purchases because I cannot buy these kinds of items. Mike challenged me at one point asking why I can buy $85 perfume and makeup, yet I can't spend $4.95 on a spoon rest! He knew the answer to that rhetorical question. The perfume and makeup are replacements. I have put off buying both until this trip because I knew I would save money on them by purchasing them here at a less expensive price. As a bonus, they are duty-free as well. They are "necessities," and they get used up and need to be replaced. As for the "necessity" part, no, they are not necessities in the same way as food, but they are in the category of "allowed" expenses.

The rule is, nothing can be bought that hasn't already been in use by me. A purchase can be made to replace what is depleted. There is no price limit on the amount that can be spent on these items, and yes, the makeup and perfume that I use are expensive. But this spending plan is not about changing how much I spend on allowable purchases. It is about not purchasing tangible items that are non-perishable to help me learn to control my impulsive spending practices and to value delayed gratification.

It is also about staying within my budget. This point is one that I am afraid I am not abiding by at all since I am not following a budget. I want to get serious about this these last not quite four months. Want to, yes. But will I? This vacation has surely tested that resolve. I have not even added up my purchases. I will do that no later than tomorrow, and "face the music."

It will not be surprising at all if it is necessary to "borrow" from next month's allowance. And then, there is Tuscany in October. If I have already "borrowed" from October, will there be anything left to spend in Tuscany?

Well, there are only approximately four months left until the end of this spending plan. I can "buckle down" and get serious about the budget, and tighten up some each month. I need/ want to get this part of the plan moving in the right direction. If I get this done, I will feel so much better about myself.

In fact, I feel better about myself already. Significant progress has already been made. Delayed gratification is occurring, and the different feeling that it creates compared to feeling out of control about spending is significant.

Now, as for my eating, I did "backslide" in that area while on vacation. I did not eat everything that I wanted, although calories nor points were a focus. I can tell that I have put on a few pounds. How many, I do not know. And that will not be clear until Monday week when I plan to weigh after having been back on the program for a week.

The good news is that I can still wear the clothes that I took with me, and they are not too tight.

Our vacation was wonderful. We are blessed to be able to vacation in the Caribbean two full weeks and to be able to take the adult children and Mary Grace with us for much of that time. I never forget that these times are memories in the making and that none of us is guaranteed anything more than the current moment.

For this, and more, feelings of gratitude abound.

And oh, our soon to be grandchild is another girl!

September 25

Well, here I am, still writing no more often than every two weeks. I guess that I will not fight this and will accept that my original plan for how often I would journal and what I am now consistently doing are somewhat different.

This is a week of cleaning and organizing the garage. We have friends from Holland arriving in a few days, as well as a friend from D.C. They will be with us for several days. Mike has few pet peeves, but one of them is a messy garage. While I clean the garage at least twice a year, between those times things just seem to accumulate there. And this cleaning is going to be different, much more extensive than most. The garage has been "housing" several pieces of furniture and smaller antique and collectible items for several months. It is time to get rid of them. The perfect opportunity for that is coming up next weekend. There is an antique sale in a nearby town where I am going to sell as much as I can, even if I have to let things go for less money than I prefer. I am tired of the mess, stress, and less I have (once again) allowed to collect, not just in the garage, but everywhere. I also am going to go through the drawers and cabinets and get rid of anything that I do not love, really use, or need. This will be hard for me, the packrat. We will see how I do.

September 26

Great progress was made on day one in cleaning the garage, yet there is so much more to do. I worked three hours this morning, but there are at least three more days of three hours each to finish this project. Thankfully, my schedule is light in the mornings this week, so I am dedicating three hours each morning to this task. The items that I am selling at the antique show will go to my office to be stored temporarily so that the garage is clean for Mike and our visitors.

September 27

I can finally see that this garage cleaning project has an end. While I committed three days to it, I did not know if I would finish once I realized the magnitude of it. But the end is in sight. I have been diligent and am even throwing out some stuff, though probably not enough. A case in point is the wooden pasta rack that I found in a cabinet. I have never used it nor have I recently used the electric pasta maker. I can't get rid of these yet, however. I am going to give myself until Thanksgiving to use them, and if not, out they go. No other option is possible if they are not used in that time! If I do use them, I will decide if I will get enough use out of them to justify keeping them.

I wish the pasta rack and pasta maker were the only items that fell into this category. It is good that I haven't bought anything for the house this year. Where could I possibly have put anything else?

I do have room for a few things, however, that I would love to have with company coming. Not to "show off," but because I do love our home and the beauty of it, and there are some items that we have not purchased since we renovated that I want us to be able to purchase when the time is right. These are clearly not "needs." Do we "need" rugs? No, not in true "need" fashion. But the wood floors will be warmer and prettier with rugs, and I will make that purchase next year. I also would like to have window treatments for the dining room and family room. Those windows are currently uncovered. They look fine, but I want some simple, elegant window treatments, not to cover the windows, but to soften the windows and bathe them in color.

But these items must wait until the new year, or later. I am sticking to my commitment not to buy anything for myself or the house this year. When I do buy them, they will not be impulse buys as have been many of my purchases in the past. They will be mindful purchases.

September 28

While I am cleaning the garage and getting rid of stuff, I am also thinking of the upcoming major transition in my life, both professional and personal. Gina has only two more days to work with me full time. She starts her new job on October 1st. I will miss her terribly. She has been such a big part of the business for six years. She has also been a big help to me and my family in a variety of ways. Gina and I blurred the boundaries of professional and personal. She has been willing to do anything that I needed her to do and has functioned in some ways as a "personal assistant." The last garage cleaning was our project, not just mine. We have polished silver together before family events. We shared helping Tara with Mary Grace when she was born. I will miss Gina more than I can find words to say. But she has decided that it is time to spread her wings in a different direction, and I am proud of her for taking the risk. I hope it is a great change for her, although I know that it will be a hard change for me. I know that I will be fine, but this major change will require that I change, and at least temporarily, do things that I do not want to do.

September 29

I am off to Alabama for what should be a fun weekend. The main reason for the trip is a party tomorrow that Pam, my 32-year friend, is having for her best "friends." I am honored to be among the twelve women so designated. I do not know what to expect other than Pam said it is a party for us. One might wonder how someone can have twelve "best friends." Be that as it may, I still feel honored. It begins with a luncheon. Pam said the event would last several hours. I am curious as to what else is involved. I will know soon!

September 30

The "best friends" party was wonderful. The luncheon was Italian, and the food was delicious. There were two types of pasta, olive bread, butternut risotto, rosemary pecans, Italian cream cake, iced tea, and tiramisu coffee. The most nourishing part of the event was not the food, however, but the individual speeches that Pam gave each one of us. Once we finished eating, Pam went around one by one and told each of us what we mean to her. She went in chronological order, beginning with the friend who is the most recent. I was number 10, followed by a friend who "beat me" by a couple of months, then Shirshee, Pam's mother, who she noted as her best girlfriend of all. It was so touching. We all cried, relishing the warm words of love and appreciation. Pam then gave each one of us a bag with our names written on it. Inside each bag were some of her favorite things. I am sure that all of the "best friends" loved their presents as much as I loved mine. But since I have not purchased any "treats" for myself this entire year, my presents from Pam were especially appreciated.

Third Quarter

Challenges and Insights

January 1, 2017

Travel, food, and weight gain continued in the third quarter of the year. My writings were certainly not "at least weekly" as I planned nor were they as lengthy as those in earlier quarters. Most likely this had as much to do with my "good at starting things, not as good at finishing them" behavior as anything else.

The importance of relationships, especially with family and close friends, was a theme again in this quarter. The connection of relationships to nurturing was reinforced with the "Best Friends" party. As I read this section, the impermanence of our time saddened me. Two of the "best friends" have passed away—Shirshee, Pam's mother who was like a mother to me, and Bonnie Jean. Shirshee died suddenly in the Spring of 2007, while I was on a second trip to Italy. I came home from that trip a day early, hoping to make it to see her before she died, but I did not get there in time. Her loss is still profound to all of us and always will be. As others will understand, the only comfort we had in losing her so quickly was the knowledge that she did not suffer long.

And yes, I did take another trip to Italy with many of the same women only six months after the Tuscany trip that occurred during the year of no spending. I probably need to be a travel writer!

The other "best friend" from Pam's party who passed away was much younger. We lost her to cancer. While not a "best friend" of mine, Bonnie Jean and her then husband were friends of mine and Troy's during our marriage. Thinking about Bonnie Jean and her death at a young age reminds me of a recent loss. A long time friend of mine, Anna, passed away suddenly when she was 59 years old. She also was lost to cancer. This was less than two months ago as I write this. Anna had lived in England the past few years, so we only saw each other once a year though that did not diminish our friendship. I saw Anna in April, having no idea that it would be the last time.

I also am thinking of another close friend of ours, Bryan Townsend, who died unexpectedly a few years ago. Mike and I were on an international business trip when we got the call about Bryan's aneurysm. We came home immediately, but did not make it before he died. Bryan and his wife Judy are my longest friends. I met them when I was only 15, fifty years ago! Bryan, Judy, and my first husband, Troy, were best friends from childhood, and we all were very close. When Troy and I divorced, Bryan, Judy, and I remained friends and brought Mike into the fold when he and I married. Through the years, we have travelled from North Carolina to Alabama several times a year, celebrating birthdays, graduations, and marriages. Pam's family, the Davis', and the Townsends are not just friends, they are family. While the physical distance from them in Alabama to us in North Carolina does not allow us to be together frequently, we have not allowed the physical distance to be an emotional distance. We have made the effort to be together.

The connections in these relationships are amazing to me. We have stayed friends through happy times and times of loss. I believe we strengthen each other. These people are so dear to me. I am going to go down memory lane a little more. For my fiftieth birthday in 2001, best friends Anna, Judy, Pam, Bryan, and Shirshee all came to St. Maarten to celebrate with me. Judy not only brought her suitcase with her clothes, she brought a second suitcase with fifty presents for me! I still have the handwritten notes that accompanied each gift and am nurtured (without food) and warmed when I reread them, as I do periodically.

Synchronicity. I am struck by the fact that as I write this, Mike and I are travelling to Alabama to see these friends. Pam and her husband Butch's first granddaughter, Ella Mae, is almost eight months old, and we have yet to see her! Pam's dad, Coy, and the rest of us aren't getting any younger so I am glad Mike and I are going now! We also will spend some time with Judy and her family. Judy's son, Jim, has cancer, and we will be able to spend some time with him and the rest of the family. And this brings me full around to the impermanence of material things and even our lives.

I am thankful that Mike, our family and close friends, and I are able to make relationships a priority. We do not know when times together will be our last time. We need to enjoy, love, and support each other in every way we can, as long as we can. These are the things that count.

Fourth Quarter 2006

October 7

Mike's dad arrived today and will be with us for two or three months. He is here for surgery, surgery that hopefully will restore him to good health. Dad had surgery in Florida in the spring, and he has not recovered to our satisfaction. After much coaxing, and Mike finding him lying in the flower bed at his house unable to get up, a condition he had been in for at least an hour, he finally agreed to come to Raleigh. His surgery and recovery will most likely extend until late January or early February. Rosie's son lives in Rhode Island and has pancreatic cancer so she will be with us when she can.

Mike and I are glad that we have the ability to help Dad and Rosie. We realize that this will be a big change for all of us.

October 13

Another "friends" event! This time it is my book club's 10th anniversary celebration, a weekend at the beach. There are ten of us in book club, and nine of us could attend our anniversary celebration. The location was at our beach, Caswell, on Oak Island, NC, which is approximately three hours from Raleigh.

We arrived Friday afternoon, checked in, and began to relax. Our dinner was a delicious homemade beef stew, an amazing salad, and wonderful crusty breads, followed by my strawberry shortcake. Saturday morning we dined on waffles and breakfast meats. Lunch was a smorgasbord of breads and spreads. Dinner was steamed shrimp, which I missed due to needing to leave early for a speech in Philadelphia the following morning.

Our time together was relaxing and fun and had little to do with books. We did briefly discuss our October book, but the weekend was more about celebrating than books. Although there are several subgroups in our book club who have traveled together, this is the first time that the entire group has planned a getaway. I doubt that I was the only one who wondered how this trip would be.

Although there is shopping close by, no one wanted to shop. There are also restaurants nearby. We had planned to eat out on Saturday night, but we found we did not want to go out at all, so we ordered in.

What did we do? Ate, slept, walked, and talked. We were nourished physically and emotionally. When that happens, the need for "stuff" lessens.

Mike did fine with Dad at home. I knew he would. I did feel a little guilty leaving them, but this trip with book club was important. It is also important for Mike to be with Dad as much as he can, when he can. With Mike's travel schedule, I will be doing a lot of the caretaking. I also have a busy travel schedule for the next few weeks—business, as well as personal—so logistics could get a little interesting!

October 14

Off to Philadelphia on an early flight for a speech. I am also doing an exhibit, showcasing my book and "It's in the Sauce!" which is my new brand. I am excited about this and a little nervous. This is potentially a very important audience for me, 1500 nursing leaders/managers. I am investing quite a lot in the exhibit. Gina is with me for this since she had committed to do this trade show prior to her decision to leave for other employment.

I have not have written much about Gina's departure. Her full-time employment with me ended on September 30th. While she is still working with me on a very part-time basis, at least until the end of the year, this change is a big one for me. Gina has been so very valuable to me. She knows me and the business so well. I am not even going to try to hire someone new until the first of the year.

I feel like I am on a roller coaster with so many changes happening.

October 18

I am on the plane headed home from Philadelphia. The speech and the exhibit were a big success! I had many people seek me out after the speech to tell me how much they enjoyed it. They also came by the booth and some bought books and tapes.

I was in the city of brotherly love for three and a half days, in the middle of downtown Philadelphia with shops all around, and I never went out of the hotel. I was focused on the business at hand and thoroughly enjoyed it.

October 19

Brenda Schell and I left today for Italy. We are on a ten-day trip with 11 other women. I only know one of the other women. I have never traveled with a group of women for this long. It should be a wonderful trip, filled with dining, shopping, and touring. I am so grateful that Mike gave me this gift. If you remember, he said it was for my birthday, Christmas, and anniversary, and probably not just this year!

This is the trip that I almost did not take. I was worried that I would not be able to shop, at least for me, and Italy is a delightful place to shop. I convinced myself that I could enjoy the trip without giving in to shopping. My shopping will only be for gifts. Surely, the cultural experience will be sufficient for a great trip. Also, hopefully, this is not the only time that I can go to Italy. There should be other opportunities.

October 20

We have arrived in Lucca, our first stop in Italy. We will be here for two nights. We arrived mid afternoon, checked into our hotel, then met the group outside on the patio for drinks, after which we walked to dinner.

The women seem interesting and fun. I am convinced it will be a good trip, even minus shopping.

October 21

This was our first full day, and it began with a walking tour of Lucca. Lucca is a lovely town. We then went to a cooking school, which was great fun and a tasty experience. After lunch, we had time for shopping. I bought a few small gifts. The gifts were for others, of course. Not too much temptation yet.

This trip through the Tuscany part of Italy was memorable. We shopped, dined on wonderful food, and enjoyed the scenery and all that the area has to offer. I found that I did not want to take the time to write in this journal, and I didn't. We were on a fast schedule, and when we returned from our excursions, I was too tired to write.

As for my purchases, I bought purses for Tara and Chatham at the Gucci outlet but nothing for myself (of course.)

October 29

After saying our goodbyes to our traveling companions at the hotel in Florence, Brenda and I are on a plane headed home. We did a one-night layover in London since Brenda had never been there.

After checking in at the hotel in the Mayfair area, we went to a pub, which is a necessary outing in London. Brenda was fine with staying there, but I wanted to introduce her to Harrods. One cannot go to London and not see Harrods.

While Harrods was interesting to Brenda, she was obviously not as enamored with it as I am. We looked around there for a while, had a bite to eat in the Tapas bar, then returned to the pub for a short while, before turning in for the evening.

The hotel is lovely although the rooms are quite small and expensive. It is foolish to pay what we paid for a few hours of sleep.

October 30

Back to Raleigh. Mike and Dad did fine without me, and Mike even became "Aga certified." Since we renovated our house a couple of years ago, I have been the one who has done most of the cooking on the Aga. It is a different kind of cooking, and Mike had not taken the time to learn all the "ins and outs" of it. Now he is proficient!

November 5

En route to the office late this afternoon to work a short while with Gina, I checked office messages and had a shock. A message had come in yesterday morning, Saturday, from the Carolina Antique Mall where I rent space, stating that the mall was closed effective immediately and that I should come pick up my stuff that day or Monday! The message said that there would be a letter at the mall explaining the situation.

I cannot imagine what has happened. The mall has been in business for many years although I have only had a space there for two years. My immediate thought is that the owner has gone bankrupt, although there has been no indication of anything of that nature. I have received my small monthly checks on time, and things appeared to be doing well. Since it is Sunday, I must wait until tomorrow to find out the details.

What will I do with the stuff in my booth? It isn't going back into the garage. I don't have room at the shop in Oak Island for anything other than what is there already. I suppose that I will inquire about another location in Raleigh, at least while I decide what to do. I do not want to make an impulsive decision just because I have to do something quickly.

Today is Mike's birthday. We plan to celebrate by going out to dinner. Unlike me, Mike does not buy much for himself. I enjoy buying for him. I often buy him clothes, which he can use and doesn't usually buy for himself.

November 6

On the way to Carolina Antique Mall, I stopped at a shop a mile from my house to see about renting a space there. It would certainly be convenient. The drawback is that is isn't an antique shop. It is a large gift shop that has a few antiques.

I talked with the manager and took an application. There are a few spaces available. The shop is lovely, but I am not sure that it is what I need other than the convenience of being close to home. The rent is expensive, more than I have been paying. Additionally, there is a twelve-month required lease commitment.

I do not think this is a good option for me. I do not need to make any more of a financial investment than I was already making. I may need to scale down and only have the shop at the beach.

But then, what will I do with all of my stuff that I must pick up?

I went to the antique shop, and the story was a problem with unpaid taxes that resulted in the closure. So sad. I now have to decide what to do with all of this stuff I had there. This is not how I need to be spending my time in November. Thanksgiving is around the corner, and I have to ready the house for our major Thanksgiving event.

Stuff is growing, although I am not buying. I am not buying for me, that is. I certainly have been buying. My gift closet is packed. I have already outspent for Christmas, in items if not in money. I also have gifts left over from last Christmas.

Have I spent more on others to satisfy the desire to shop? I do not think so. My desire isn't to shop; it's for beautiful things.

How can it be almost Christmas again? This year has flown by. It is hard to believe that I have less than two months to go on my year of no spending.

There are some items that are desperately in need of being replaced and not just the jacket I wrote about earlier. I am in sore need of undergarments. Replacing them truly would be classified as a need. But I am too close to the end of the year to buy anything now, although I could justify doing so for business purposes. I do not want to, however.

I want to finish this year without having purchased anything for myself. This will be a major accomplishment.

Now, where is Oprah? It's time to get my PR staff working on getting me on Oprah! I have lessons about this experience to share with others!

There has been no temptation to shop these past few days. My focus has been on figuring out what to do with all of this stuff from the antique shop.

November 13

This is the last week to prepare for family coming for Thanksgiving. For most of the past twenty years, we have had Thanksgiving at our home in Raleigh. Family comes down from Maryland and up from Florida, some arriving the weekend before the holiday and the last leaving the weekend after. Most everyone is in town by Tuesday, and there are meals to prepare from Wednesday through Saturday.

While I in no way do all of the cooking, there are many other preparations to be made. All beds in the house are in use, as well as sofas and even pallets on the floor for younger children. One of the older children's favorite stories is the transition from the pallets on the floor to a bed! There are other family members with homes in town who also house some relatives and some stay in rental places.

It is a special time of food, fellowship, and memories. We usually have forty to forty-five relatives together for several days. We will have at least that many this year. In earlier years, I thought that I had to do everything myself, including most of the cooking, but that changed years ago when I was not present for our Thanksgiving tradition. That year I had a request to speak at Montreal General Hospital in Montreal, Canada on our Thanksgiving. Canada and the U.S. do not share the same Thanksgiving holiday. I was very torn. I wanted to do the speech, but I also did not want to leave my family on this important holiday.

Mike made that ok for me. He told me to go. He said Thanksgiving could go on without me (ouch!) and that he would organize and coordinate the events, and others would help. And organize and coordinate he did, and others helped in a major way. Mike, unlike me, is great at delegating. Cooking and chore lists were developed, and our family has never returned to me trying to do it all. I learned a valuable lesson from this. When others are fully included, they are fully engaged. That year Thanksgiving became ours, truly a family event.

November 20

Not shopping this month is not difficult; there are so many other things to do. I finally have the house fairly ready for company to arrive for Thanksgiving, although there are always some last minute things to be done. I actually never feel I am as ready as I want to be when the first guests arrive, but I have to let what hasn't been done go and enjoy the family.

November 27

Well, another Thanksgiving is in the history books. As usual, it was a wonderful time. The next event is my birthday, which some years comes during the turkey holiday, but it is a few days later this year. Then next weekend, some of the family are coming back to spend some time with Dad.

December 1

Our niece and nephew, Lisa and Rob, and Rob's children, Sam and Halle, came in for the weekend, especially to spend some time with Dad. We had a wonderful visit. One of the weekend's activities was working on a major puzzle, which we did complete. I plan to frame it.

December 2

Sam, Halle, and I went Christmas tree shopping today. We always have at least two live trees and sometimes three. I purchased two live trees for this year's Christmas holiday. Since live trees do not live for the next year so they can be used again,

I considered this purchase in the category of "disposables." I was perfectly ok with this purchase and do not think that it was outside of my commitment to not purchase anything for the house.

December 4

Oh, no! I just realized that while my purchase of Christmas trees was not a violation of my no-spending commitment, buying two Christmas tree stands was! I did not even think of this at the time. For whatever reason, I just made this connection today.

When Sam, Halle, and I went to buy the trees, I had forgotten to take my tree stands with me so the guys could put the trees in the stands. At the time, I did not even think about going home to get the stands; all I thought about was what a hassle it would be if the trees were not put in the stands and Mike had to do it. Also, the tree stands that the tree lot had for purchase were nicer and looked easier to use than the ones we had at home, so I thought it made sense to upgrade our stands. I had the sellers put the trees in the stands and load everything into our van. I paid the bill, and we headed home. Decorating the trees will be done in a few days. I never even thought about the fact that buying these tree stands was a violation of my no-spending commitment. This was clearly an impulse buy, made without thinking. Since I had not planned ahead, I had a dilemma that I resolved by spending money and convincing myself that it was a good purchase, that these tree stands were better than the ones we had.

With my year of no spending almost over, I made the purchase of two tree stands, the only non-allowable purchase that I have made all year. With this purchase, I violated my commitment not to purchase any (non-disposables) for me or the house all year. With less than a month to go, lack of planning (not taking my tree stands with me to the tree lot) and impulsivity (purchasing new ones) resulted in this. If I had planned to violate my no-spending commitment, it would not have been to purchase tree stands!

How easy it is to spend, even when we are committed NOT to, when we are not being mindful of what we are doing.

December 5

I drove to Atlanta today for a client visit at Auburn University. I spent the night with Tara, Stephen, and Mary Grace. Before leaving for the trip, I readied the house for Christmas since they will be driving back with me for the weekend. I took a bag of Christmas items that I have not used for several years, thinking Tara might want them. They are still in good condition, but colors I no longer use. Tara said what she does not want, she will take to Goodwill.

December 23, 2006

Our annual Christmas breakfast was quite a success. 51 people came, and they were all seated for a wonderful meal. A friend, Carolyn, was amazed at that, asking where all of that stuff, china, chairs, etc. is at other times. If she only knew how much moving in and out of tables and chairs Gina and I do between the office, antique shop, and storage shed! I have more than enough "stuff" for parties, and it is "stuff." Although I do love entertaining and all its accoutrements, the joy of entertaining to me is in the fellowship with family and friends more than the beauty of the tables. At least I think that is the truth. But if it is, why did I tell Mike that I need more Christmas china? I don't "need" anything other than relationships and enough financial means to pay for those things that are important to me.

We seated 44 adults and seven children, all with proper china and silver. We have 20 Christmas plates. I added more Christmas décor on the tables set with other china. While I would like more Christmas china, I certainly do not "need" it. However, I would like some blue Christmas china, although I have not seen a blue Christmas pattern that I like. Mike has given me all of the Christmas china as gifts through the years. When I told him that I would like more Christmas china, he said, "Not this year."

Maureen, her mom Bernadette, and I went to Southern Season this afternoon. I purchased some stocking stuffers for Mike and some food items. There were many other things to buy in that wonderful store, some of which I would have undoubtedly purchased in a different year. But not this year!

December 24

Most of the last two days were spent preparing for the Christmas breakfast and Christmas. On Friday, I spent all of the waking hours, (and some hours that I should have been asleep) cooking, setting tables, and readying the house for the Christmas breakfast.

This year with the Christmas breakfast a day before Christmas Eve, the afternoon was more pleasant for me. Most years the breakfast is on Christmas Eve and that day also involves a Christmas Eve dinner for family and close friends. Years that Christmas Eve falls on Sunday, the breakfast is held on Saturday, so as not to interfere with church.

Mike and I agreed that this year's breakfast was our best ever in several ways. I was more prepared and therefore able to enjoy the event, which was not always the case in past years. The tables were placed better, so traffic flow was not a problem. Although there were more different types of food, it was all ready on time and, according to our guests, it was all delicious. This is a much easier schedule for me with those two meals being on different days. I think I will routinely schedule the breakfast on December 23rd, although some people might not be able to attend since they may still be working. Our neighbors make so many heartwarming comments about this tradition of ours, saying it puts them in the Christmas spirit.

December 25

We had a wonderful but quiet day at home until the evening. We slept in later than usual with no small children to wake us up earlier. We took our time opening presents before having a leisurely breakfast.

Just as Mike had promised, Santa brought me fewer gifts this year due to my main gift being my October trip to Tuscany. I did get some Thanksgiving china—four Thanksgiving plates in a new pattern. I now have more Thanksgiving china than Christmas china. I had several gifts from others, including from Tara, Chatham, and Dad and Rosie. All seemed happy with their gifts from me, which made me happy!

December 26

Yesterday, Christmas day, ended on a pleasant note with dinner at a friend's. Christmas day is usually a day filled with relaxation and good meals. It is one of only a couple of days in the year we enjoy like this. With all of the activity on Thanksgiving Day and the days leading up to Christmas, not shopping on Christmas Day was no challenge, even if I could have found an open store.

It is too early to tell how retailers did this year. In our area it has been unseasonably warm, so many retailers have been deep discounting winter clothes and other cold weather items. I hope those deep discounts are still in effect in January.

Today, we went to Joe and Mary's for chili. Joe is Mike's brother and lives in town. Steve—another of Mike's brothers—and his family came from Florida. We snacked, had lunch, and sat around for several hours afterward just talking. I know how important it is to be able to sit and relax and have nothing else to do but that, and yet it is something that I rarely do. As the day wore on, I began to wonder at what point it would be appropriate to depart. Steve and his family would be driving to Carolina Beach, an almost three-hour drive. Since our drive was only 30 minutes, it seemed rude to "need" to leave before they did. As the day wore on, I could see that Dad and Mike were both getting quite restless. None of us had anything else that we needed to be doing, but sitting for hours seemed to be difficult. I was struck by the thought of how few times we have the luxury of just sitting, relaxing, and having conversation. Maybe the fact that it is so rare is one of the reasons that it is so hard to do.

December 27

I haven't done any after Christmas shopping this year. A sister-in-law told me that there is blue Christmas china on sale at HomeGoods. I will go and look at it next week to see if it is still there. I am not sure that I will purchase any, even if I like it. I am considering my shopping goals for next year. I am not yet sure what they will be, but I want to reinforce the shopping lessons learned this year. Buying more Christmas china might not be consistent with those goals.

I did some cleaning out of closets today, especially Tara's closet. When I travel to Georgia tomorrow, I will take quite a bit of that with me. I do not want to choose what to keep and what to discard of her "treasures." She has ample closet space to store these items if she is not able to go through them in the next few days.

I also have a pile of stuff to take to Goodwill before the end of the year. That pasta machine that I promised to use before Thanksgiving or discard is still in a cabinet, unused. While I did not use the pasta machine before Thanksgiving, I decided that I could not ("would not," more aptly spoken) get rid of it yet. There are many items that I have disposed of, even items that I like and think I might use at some point. But there is something about the pasta machine that is different. Maybe it is the recent trip to Italy and the desire to make homemade pasta. I want to hold onto the pasta machine a little longer.

December 28

I am one day shy of the exact time in 2005 when I made my commitment not to spend anything on myself or the house in all of 2006. It is amazing to me that now it seems this year has gone so quickly. I know at some points in the year, it seemed it was dragging on forever.

In only four days, I will be able to spend again. I am making a mental list of my desired purchases. There are some purchases that I want/need to make. Some of those are for personal items that do not need to be identified, but that do need to be replaced. I have been struggling for several months with needing to replace some of these. While I have more of these items than what I am replacing, the weight that I have gained again has resulted in some of those not fitting well. Because of this, I may wait until the end of January to make this purchase and allow myself time to lose some weight. I do not want to purchase something on January 1 that I hope will *not* fit me on January 31. I will see how this weight reduction plan transpires before making a final decision about this purchase.

I have several conflicting emotions about this year ending. I am proud and excited that with one exception (the previously noted Christmas tree stands), I have kept this commitment I made to myself. There have been times when I certainly was tempted to stray from the plan, but my resolve to stay committed was greater than the temptation. The only purchase that I made was a total accident. It was a couple of days before I realized what I had done. Had I realized it at the time, I would have tried to return the items. Since two days had passed before I realized what I had done, it was too late to return the tree stands. The trees were already soaking up water in the stands. This accidental spending in the midst of my major commitment reinforced to me how mindless spending can be. Of all of the items I *wanted* to purchase this year, tree stands were never on the list!

One of my most valuable lessons this year has been how easy it is to avoid spending when you have made a commitment. The word "commitment" is the operative word. A commitment is stronger than a decision. I have made similar decisions related to money before. So what was different this time? Perhaps those were just decisions, not commitments. Or, perhaps at least some of those were commitments, but not of the magnitude of this commitment. This commitment was so huge that it required focus and discipline at a much higher level than anything that I had done previously. Another difference is that I had "told the world"! Several people verbalized that there is no way that I could do this for an entire year. Their lack of faith was not as strong as my commitment!

A strong feeling in addition to the excitement and pride is fear. I fear that I will revert to my old ways of mindless spending. At the beginning of this year, I wrote that I would not do that, that the pain of this commitment would not be worth it if the lessons learned did not last. Intellectually, I do believe that will be the case. Emotionally, I am scared, for I know that old habits do not die easily or quickly. This feels somewhat like being an alcoholic, when the first drink leads to many others. Will the fact that I will be able to spend again on items I have not purchased for a year start the cycle all over again? I certainly hope not, and I plan not. I must assure that such does not happen. I am thinking of a way to prevent myself from falling back into bad spending habits.

Another of my most valuable lessons this year is how often I find things that I think I have lost, just by letting time pass and not being able to purchase another item when I have "lost" something. A recent example is hairspray. Hairspray is a disposable, so I have been able to purchase replacement hairspray. Since Mike and I have moved all over the house the past few months while others have been staying with us, it has been easy to misplace things. Just this morning I found my favorite hairspray under the bathroom sink where I had put it days ago while cleaning up for company. When I misplaced it, instead of going out and purchasing more, I used a less desirable hairspray for those days. I knew I had not lost my favorite hairspray permanently, but I was certainly frustrated for those days that it was missing!

I realized from this example, as well as from other examples this year, that my failure to deal effectively with minor frustrations, especially not wanting to wait, has resulted in me buying things in the past that I did not need. There are other examples of this. But this year I have made different decisions. One of those decisions was to use a hair product that I did not really like instead of purchasing a different kind. I decided that there was more value in using what I had, even if I did not like it, than spending money I did not need to spend. In this lesson is also the awareness that I sometimes have bought things just for a change when what I was using was perfectly satisfactory. This year I wanted to use up what I had before buying replacement items. It feels good to be successful in this.

December 29

Tara, Mary Grace, and I went shopping this afternoon. Tara needed to buy some last minute Christmas presents for family she would be visiting. We went to Tuesday Morning, a discount home goods store. I enjoyed looking and bought a couple of gifts. I bought our soon-to-be-born granddaughter (due late January/early February) an outfit. I also bought a small gift for our gift closet. I saw several items that I would have liked to have that were reasonably priced. When I can purchase items again early next week, I may go to Tuesday Morning and buy a trivet that is expandable. I discarded several trivets last week that I no longer use. Since I love to cook and entertain, trivets come in handy. (I almost said, "that I need" a trivet, but I know that "need" is not really the case.)

Tara, Mary Grace, and I had a relaxing day. We selected pictures of Mary Grace and others, (but mainly of Mary Grace!) for Tara and Stephen's 2007 calendar. We did that online and would have ordered the calendar except we were missing a couple of photos that we need to find before completing the calendar.

It is hard to believe that Mary Grace is almost two years old and that her sister is soon to arrive. As I looked at the pictures of the last year, I am amazed at how quickly babies change. It is similar to how fast this year of no spending has passed. I hope that my changes will be as significant as Mary Grace's.

December 30

This turned out to be another day of shopping, although again, I did not spend anything, other than for lunch. Tara, Mary Grace, and I went to Lenox Mall to have lunch with Tara's friend, Kathryn, and her girls Claire and Elise. The children were precious. After lunch Tara, Mary Grace, and I looked around the mall for quite awhile, looking at baby things especially. Mary Grace thoroughly enjoyed playing in The Pottery Barn Kids kitchen. I am very excited about the kitchen we bought for Mary Grace for Christmas and can hardly wait for Stephen to get home this evening to set it up. Mike (Dr. Danks) spent many hours putting it together for her. I wish he could see her play with it, but he stayed behind in Raleigh to care for Dad.

Stephen and his friend Scott brought the kitchen in and set it up in the family room. Mary Grace went right to it and started playing like a kitchen pro. It is amazing to me how children learn so quickly. Mary Grace insisted that Tara, Stephen, and I sit down and play with her. I would do well to spend more time playing.

December 31

Well, this is it; the last day of the year! I know that I have said it before, but I must say it one more time. It is amazing to me that an entire year has passed. I know that the adage "the older we get, the faster it goes" is true. Still, I was not prepared for how fast this year would pass. Of course, there were times that it did not seem to pass quickly at all. But as I look back on this year, it is amazing to me that I have not purchased anything for me or the house (other than the tree stands) for an entire year. I did it. I kept the commitment I made to myself.

I spent the early part of today driving from Douglasville, Georgia, to Raleigh. It rained most of the day, which made the drive seem longer. I had a lot of time to think and reflect on this year.

What are my lessons from this experience? While some have been previously noted, here are my main lessons:

- Time passes so quickly, both when we are in control and especially when we aren't.

- When I make a commitment, not just set plans or goals, amazing things happen.

- Impulsive buying accounted for much of my spending in the past.

- When I am focused on not buying, I can be successful in controlling my spending. The "not buying" mindset works!

- Large goals (commitments) result in a firm resolve and a growing desire to succeed.

I have always made New Year's Resolutions, but like so many resolutions, those New Year's Resolutions are forgotten before January ends. This commitment not to buy anything for myself or the house for a full year was without a doubt my greatest test yet, and my greatest success. I will not say that it is my greatest commitment, for my commitment to my marriage and my family gets that award. I must affirm, however, that had I not made a commitment, had I just set a goal or made a plan, I most likely would not have been successful.

Commitments are so much stronger than decisions, goals, or plans. This has spurred me on to set an overarching commitment for upcoming years. As I began this year, one of my reasons for making this commitment was to "be the change you wish to see in the world" (credit to Gandhi). This was related to my desire to live the tagline from my business: "Inspiring Positive Change." I do not yet know if this change of mine will inspire anyone else at all, but I do know that it has inspired me. It is important to me that I live a life congruent to the message I teach in my business practice so that I can help others. Gandhi would certainly think this congruence was important.

So, what will it be for the new year? While I am sure that I have spent less total money in this year than I did in previous years, I don't have the numbers to show the results. I have never been good at keeping up with the numbers, any numbers, specifically dollars or points, and this year is no exception. This has been a lifelong problem for me, and I have not conquered the problem this year.

So, one of my disappointments this year is that I consistently failed to live within a budget, although I had planned to create and follow one. (That may be the problem; that part was a plan, not a commitment.) I told myself that I would manage my money better by living within a budget. In essence, I would count money as well as calories and points. Well, if you read carefully, you will see the holes in that. While it is clear to me that when I am focused on managing money and weight, I am more successful. But I am also clear about the fact that doing this is against my norm. It was too easy to get busy and kid myself into thinking that I could keep those numbers and points in my head. That does not work for me.

So, a worthwhile goal for the coming year is to daily and consistently manage my money and my weight. To do so will require great discipline. I need to establish a budget for my spending and stay within it. I also need to manage my weight and not go into another year twenty pounds overweight. I need to stop the yo-yo syndrome.

So, I have a new *commitment* starting tomorrow. That commitment will include continuing the progress made in this year. My spending must be different than it was before this year of major change or I will be right back where I started, or even worse. My spending needs to be much more purposeful and less impulsive.

I will also make and live within a budget. I have learned from this year that failure to do so drastically affects my ability to manage my money. While I have learned that when I make a commitment, I can be successful, I have also learned that there are strategies that help me keep my commitments. One of these strategies is a budget.

Goodbye to this year, and hello to a new year of a new me!

I hope that you have found some value in following my journey. If so, I am glad. I wish you well with all of your commitments!

Fourth Quarter

Challenges and Insights

January 1, 2017

Although I have not done a word or page count, it seems that the fourth quarter writings are the sparsest of all. By that time in that year, I think I was tired of the writing process. Also, since I did not have any specific schedule or process for the writings, it was easy to let other things, such as life and holidays, get in the way. This quarter has two major holidays, and there were preparations for both that took a considerable amount of time.

Speaking of holidays, it has always been clear to me that I place a high priority on traditions. My holiday preparations are an example of that. The family Thanksgiving event that we have hosted for all but two of the last thirty years is a tradition that I hold dear to my heart. The reason that it is so important to me likely has to do with not remembering family meals and celebrations as a child.

When Mike and I met, married, and blended our families, our traditions began, and they continue to this day. Last year and this year, our Thanksgiving holiday included 60 people, all seated at tables set with mainly Thanksgiving china and silver. Dad, who is now 93, still makes the trips, as does most of Mike's family. My family is small, and since we have not stayed close, few of those with us are from my nuclear or related family.

The exception to that is my first cousin Paula and her family who live in Raleigh, as well as her extended family through her husband Bryan. Paula is more like a daughter to me than a cousin. Another regular from my family is Uncle Barry. I mentioned in the journal entries that he and my aunt (my mother's sister) cared for me some of my early years. Uncle Barry lives a few hours from us. He has been an imprtant figure in my life, so it is wonderful to have him with us several times a year.

Relationships, traditions, and celebrations, all creating memories. When our loved ones are gone, it will be our memories and photos (although too often the photos are now still on our smart phones!) that we will have.

One more thought about Thanksgiving. Elsewhere in the journal, I said I think the beauty of the tables is less important to me than the relationships with those around the table, but I also think the beauty of the tables is more important to me than all the food for the meal!

We have not hosted a Christmas Eve breakfast for several years now. I am surprised that I who have difficulty letting go of traditions could give this up, but I did. I do miss it, but each year I am reminded that we only have so much time to spend and sometimes choices have to be made on how to spend our time. As our family grew, our family traditions grew with them. My time is now spent more on family gatherings.

Daughter Tara seems to have taken up the Christmas tradition. This year all of our nuclear family travelled to Georgia for Christmas, and Tara did all the hosting and cooking. That allowed me to spend time doing what I enjoy, making the tables beautiful!

But just for the record, the neighborhood holiday tradition did not entirely go away—one of our neighbors now hosts a holiday party!

In this quarter, I was honest about the commitments I did not keep, especially budgeting and weight control. It pains me to admit this is still the case. I have yet to make and live within a budget. The same is true for weight control. I did lose 32 pounds once since 2006. I kept it off for a while, but I found 23 of those pounds again. You already have read that today is a new day for me in this regard. I have begun the weight loss journey once more.

I am not sure about the budget. I have not yet committed to a budget, although I do want to. "Wants" are not the same as commitments. If the year of no personal spending taught me nothing else, it would have been worth it learning that. It did teach me other things though. I learned that when I plan ahead, it is easier not to spend money and even to save money. And I learned that while I often save small amounts of money, too often I waste larger amounts with things like credit card debt and buying clothes and other items that I never get around to wearing or using. Those were all big realizations for me.

Per my pattern, I have difficulty finishing things, but it is time to put this writing to rest. But not before one last comment, one final confession.

I still have that pasta machine and pasta rack, and they have not been used even once in these ten years!

About the Author

Patti Fralix is founder and president of the Fralix Group, Inc., a leadership firm specializing in individual, team, and organizational excellence. Patti speaks, consults, and coaches on leadership, customer service, and managing differ-ences for a variety of clients and audiences.

In 1993, after a 20-year career in health care, Patti started her business to live her pas-sion: inspiring positive change in work, life, and family.

Patti has published exten-sively in national publications, and her first book, *How to Thrive in Spite of Mess, Stress and Less!,* was published in 2002. She has an undergraduate degree from the University of Virginia and a master's degree from the University of Alabama in Birmingham.

Patti has a weekly blog, ***Itsinthesauce.com***. Patti and her husband Mike live in Raleigh, North Carolina.